Passover Lite

KOSHER COOKBOOK

Passover Lite
KOSHER COOKBOOK

Gail Ashkanazi-Hankin

Foreword by
Rabbi Josef A. Davidson

PELICAN PUBLISHING COMPANY
Gretna 1997

First printing, March 1996
Second printing, June 1997

Library of Congress Cataloging-in-Publication Data

Ashkanazi-Hankin, Gail.
    Passover lite kosher cookbook / Gail Ashkanazi-Hankin ; foreword
by Rabbi Josef A. Davidson.
        p.   cm.
    Includes index.
    ISBN 1-56554-133-2 (hardcover : alk. paper)
    1. Passover cookery. 2. Low-fat diet—Recipes. 3. Low
-cholesterol diet—Recipes. 4. Low-calorie diet—Recipes.
I. Title.
TX739.2.P37A85 1996
641.5'676437—dc20

                                                    95-50597
                                                        CIP

Illustrations by the author

Manufactured in the United States of America

Published by Pelican Publishing Company, Inc.
1101 Monroe Street, Gretna, Louisiana 70053

*To the future good health
and happy Passovers of my children,
Jennifer and Michael*

Contents

Foreword

Passover is one of the most memorable holidays in the entire Jewish calendar. It is certainly one of the most universally celebrated home festivals. Nearly everyone who retains any Jewish identity at all makes or finds a seder through which to experience our ancestors' journey from slavery to freedom.

Passover also fills many with anxiety—anxiety over the seder itself, the order of the service that accompanies the wonderful meal; anxiety over the types of food that are considered "leaven" and thus forbidden for the duration of the holiday; anxiety over the radical manner in which one's diet seems to have to change in order to accommodate the festival.

Leading the seder is not all that difficult. There is a wonderful guide to the seder, *Haggadah Shel Pesach* (the Passover Haggadah). One anxiety relieved!

With this cookbook, some of those anxieties will be relieved. Nothing in any of these recipes is forbidden to be consumed on Passover. All of the ingredients may be purchased "kosher for Passover" or are kosher for Passover in their fresh state. Every recipe will turn out to be absolutely delicious. Two anxieties relieved!

During Passover, many are concerned with the high cholesterol that traditional foods for this season contain, especially as eggs are a major ingredient in so many Passover recipes. Because many of the lower-fat items one might ordinarily substitute for butter, eggs, shortening, cheese, or cream contain "leaven," it is difficult for many who are concerned with the amount of fat to really enjoy Passover—until now. This cookbook will offer the reader low-fat alternatives that are not only healthy and tasty, but also kosher for Passover.

So, don't be anxious. This year enjoy Passover as never before. Be free not only of the oppression of slavery in Egypt but of the traditional high-fat, high-cholesterol menus of Passovers past. When the Israelites left Egypt, they had to cook light. This cookbook brings the holiday full circle with a lighter, lower-fat approach. This year confidently declare, "Let all who are hungry, come and eat" and enjoy!

RABBI JOSEF A. DAVIDSON
B'nai Zion Synagogue
Chattanooga, Tennessee

9

Acknowledgments

This book is the culmination of ten years of cooking, tasting, testing, perfecting, writing, rewriting, editing, typing, retyping, proofreading, and correcting. A number of friends and family members have helped me with each of these steps and my heartfelt thanks goes out to them all.

To Annette Finesilver for her encouragement to stop talking about writing a cookbook someday and to actually make the dream come true.

To my recipe testers: Ed and Anita Galemba, Sherre Kozloff, Bobbi Parris, Sally Nadel, and Sheryl Goodman—thanks for testing Passover recipes at all times of the year.

To my parents, Bernard and Bernice Ashkanazi, who also tested recipes, but who began encouraging me many years ago when I started modifying recipes for my dad, who lives with numerous food allergies.

To my husband, Larry Hankin, who lent his skills as an editor and typist to make reams of recipes into a manuscript, for his special love and support.

To my grandmother, Libbie Tecklin, who followed my progress on this book all these years but did not live to see it published.

And finally to my dear daughter, Jennifer, and son, Michael, who also encouraged me to write a cookbook and who have been tasting my creations for years. Thank-you, kids, for your honesty and for hanging in there with me.

Introduction

These recipes have been developed for those who wish to maintain their healthy style of eating and cooking while observing the Passover dietary traditions. Why undo all those months of watching calories, fat, and cholesterol with a week of heavy matzah dishes and dozens of whole eggs?

These recipes are reduced in calories, fat, sugar, and cholesterol and use wholesome, fresh ingredients as well as products that are available for Passover. The source of the nutritional analyses following each recipe is *Micro Cookbook 4.0 for Windows* (Pinpoint Publishing, 1993).

By taking full advantage of fruits and vegetables during Passover, you'll be able to replenish some of the fiber your body needs, since legumes and grains—major sources of fiber—are forbidden.

An added benefit of cooking "lite" during Passover is the relatively low cost of natural and wholesome foods. A hearty and appetizing meal doesn't have to be expensive or high in fat. Many combinations of herbs, spices, yogurt, fruits, and vegetables are not only permissible during Passover, they are essential ingredients for tasty, healthy meals that cost far less to prepare than those relying upon processed Passover products.

Are you afraid of missing the convenience of processed Passover foods? Not to worry . . . food processors and microwave ovens help save time. It is worth the extra expense to invest in a set of food processor attachments that are for Passover only.

Since dietary customs vary from family to family and from community to community, I have written this book to fit most levels of observance. Pick and choose what you feel comfortable with; there is something here for everyone. This book includes healthy versions of traditional dishes as well as contemporary, eclectic, and multiethnic recipes, all within the Passover dietary traditions and healthful guidelines.

This book is "vegetarian-friendly." With the exception of "Chicken, Turkey, and Beef," every chapter contains recipes that can be mixed and matched to create healthy yet fulfilling *pesadige* (kosher for Passover) meals. And for easy meal planning, all recipes are designated as meat, dairy, or pareve.

This book is really just a lesson in reforming your Passover cooking habits, steaming vegetables, and reducing the amount of oil and egg yolks in favorite recipes. This can be your blueprint for a new tradition, for a truly healthy and happy Passover.

Note: Among the illustrations included in this book are icons that indicate if a recipe serves as a good snack or lunch. Also, a "hamsa" icon appears with certain recipes to indicate that the recipe is a Sephardic rather than Ashkenazic recipe.

Cooking Tips

- Invest in nonstick skillets, griddles, cookie or baking sheets, and saute pans. This reduces the amount of fat you need for cooking.

- Kojel, Victors, William J. Elwood, and V.I.P. Delite all have sugar-free flavored gelatin products and pudding mixes that are kosher for Passover.

- Take advantage of colors and textures to enhance the appeal of your meals.

- Avoid most processed Passover convenience foods. These often contain saturated fats, and many do not list the percentage of saturated fat on the label. High fat is one of the most dangerous American dietary habits, and fat easily sneaks into readily available Passover foods such as cookies, brownies, candies, kugel, and stuffing mixes. In recent years, the kosher food industry has begun responding to the need for health-conscious Passover convenience foods. Such products include yolk-free Passover noodles; fat-free salad dressings; Passover egg substitutes; and gefilte fish with no sugar, less sodium, no matzah meal, and no egg yolks. Save time and enjoy!

- Having said that about convenience food, on a hectic day, you might still want to take advantage of the different flavors of canned tomato sauces that are now available. Just be aware that they sometimes contain cottonseed oil and are high in sodium, so you may want to use these products in moderation.

- Mother's has kosher-for-Passover olive oil cooking spray available. This will be very useful for many recipes and will be referred to as "cooking spray."

- If kosher-for-Passover cooking spray is not available to you or you want to save money, pour monounsaturated or polyunsaturated oil into a spray bottle to make your own cooking spray.

- Grapeseed oil is available and is low in saturated fat.

- Contrary to popular belief, honey, molasses, and brown sugar are not healthier substitutes for sugar. As with whole eggs—you don't have to omit sugar completely, just use it conservatively. Some companies have aspartame and low-calorie liquid sweetener available for Passover. In dessert recipes in which there is no heating, you can substitute the sugar with one of these products.

- Egg substitute: There is egg substitute on the market that is kosher for Passover. Use ¼ cup in place of one whole egg or two egg whites if you desire.

- Fresh herbs for Passover are best to enliven Passover recipes, but if they are not available, buy a new jar of pure dried herbs and substitute ½ to 1 teaspoon dried herbs for 1 tablespoon fresh herbs. According to the "Rabbinical Assembly Pesach Guide" brochure, unopened packages or containers of natural spices "require no kosher le Pesach label if purchased prior to Pesach."

- If you can't find a lean ground turkey that is kosher for Passover, grind your own or use a food processor. To remove as much fat as possible from the ground beef, crumble it and cook it in a nonstick skillet, then rinse the ground beef with warm water.

Time-Saving Tips

There are many quick and easy dishes in this collection. There are also dishes for people who don't mind taking the extra care and time.

If you work, you need to plan well for this week. Look through this book and assemble a basic menu plan and shop for the food to go with it.

- Prepare recipes such as Pickled Vegetables and Forty Years in the Desert Trail Mix as soon as your kitchen is ready for Passover.

- Salad can be kept fresh for about a week. This can save you a step in preparation if the lettuce is stored properly. Wash the lettuce greens whole in cold water. Shake out and dry with paper towels or a salad spinner. Wrap a dry dish towel around the lettuce leaves or place a paper towel in the bottom of a plastic container or plastic bag before storing greens in it. To serve, break up lettuce into bite-sized pieces.

- Chop three or more onions and place in a tightly covered container or small individual containers and store in the refrigerator.

- Mince garlic and ginger and freeze in a covered container. (½ tsp garlic = 1 clove)

- Buy fresh herbs ahead of time and freeze in a plastic bag.

- Green, yellow, and red peppers can be destemmed with white membranes and seeds removed then sliced into strips. Individual peppers can be stored in individual bags. Red peppers can be roasted ahead of time. Cut into strips and store in a plastic bag.

It takes some preparation to save time during the week, but the payback of a lean, healthy week for busy people is worth it.

ABBREVIATIONS

STANDARD

tsp.	=	teaspoon			
tbsp.	=	tablespoon			
oz.	=	ounce			
qt.	=	quart			
lb.	=	pound			

METRIC

ml.	=	milliliter
l.	=	liter
g.	=	gram
kg.	=	kilogram
mg.	=	milligram

STANDARD-METRIC APPROXIMATIONS

⅛ teaspoon	=	.6 milliliter		
¼ teaspoon	=	1.2 milliliters		
½ teaspoon	=	2.5 milliliters		
1 teaspoon	=	5 milliliters		
1 tablespoon	=	15 milliliters		
4 tablespoons	=	¼ cup	=	60 milliliters
8 tablespoons	=	½ cup	=	118 milliliters
16 tablespoons	=	1 cup	=	236 milliliters
2 cups	=	473 milliliters		
2½ cups	=	563 milliliters		
4 cups	=	946 milliliters		
1 quart	=	4 cups	=	.94 liter

SOLID MEASUREMENTS

½ ounce	=	15 grams		
1 ounce	=	25 grams		
4 ounces	=	110 grams		
16 ounces	=	1 pound	=	454 grams

Passover Lite

KOSHER COOKBOOK

Getting Ready for the Seder

SEDER MEAL SUGGESTIONS

FIRST-NIGHT SEDER

Ashkenazic Charoses

Appetizer

Jerusalem Platter
Lean Gefilte Fish Loaf garnished with lettuce, cooked carrots, and Chraine
(Horseradish)

Soup

Mom's Chicken Soup
with
The Lighter Matzah Balls

Main Course

Paprika Oven-Fried Chicken
Potato Puffs
Asparagus with Flair

Dessert

Fresh Fruit Salad
Cocoa Meringues
or
Strawberry Angel Food Cake with Strawberry Sauce
Decaffeinated coffee or tea

Second-Night Seder

Ashkenazic Charoses or Algerian Charoset

Appetizer
Steamed Artichokes with dip or dressing

Soup
Sweet and Sour Beet Borscht

Main Course
Roast Turkey Breast
Mushrooms Sauteed in Wine
Mixed Vegetable Kugel

Dessert
Instant Raspberry Sorbet
No Cholesterol Chocolate Chiffon Cake
Decaffeinated coffee or tea

Vegetarian Seder

Algerian Charoset

Appetizer

Mediterranean Eggplant Salad
with
Matzah Snack Crackers

Soup

Vegetarian "Chicken" Soup
with
The Lighter Matzah Balls

Main Course

Artichokes with Matzah Stuffing
Simple Pineapple Carrots
Cauliflower Kugel

Dessert

Cinnamon Chocolate Cake Roll
Berry Frozen Yogurt
Decaffeinated coffee or tea

Sephardic Seder

Algerian Charoset

Appetizer

Boulette de Poisson
with
Horseradish (Chraine)

Soup

Mom's Chicken Soup with Lemon
with
The Lighter Matzah Balls

Main Course

Chicken with Olives
Joelle's Algerian Carrots
Steamed rice with saffron
or
Egg yolk-free Passover noodles
Asparagus with sesame seeds

Dessert

Golden Macaroons
Candied Fruit Balls
Mint tea

HORSERADISH (CHRAINE)

*I make a big batch of this because my family happens to love
a little gefilte fish with their horseradish.*

**½-¾ lb. horseradish root, peeled
and cut into chunks**

**1 large beet, peeled
½ cup cider vinegar**

In a food processor, grate the horseradish and beets. Mix in the vinegar. Chop it further in the food processor for a finer consistency. Makes approximately 1½ cups.

Variation: If it's too hot, sometimes for the kids, I grate 1 medium apple with a small beet. This sweetens the horseradish naturally without adding sugar.

Calories—10; Saturated fat—0 g.; Total fat—0 g.; Carbohydrates—2 g.; Cholesterol—0 mg.; Sodium—3 mg.

ASHKENAZIC CHAROSES

*This is what Mom always used to make—
plain and simple—just like her mother did.*

3 large red apples
¼ cup chopped pecans
1 tsp. cinnamon

1 tbsp. honey
¼ cup raisins
2-3 tbsp. sweet red Passover wine

Finely chop the apples and pecans together. Stir in the remaining ingredients until well mixed. Makes approximately 3½ cups.

Variation: If you want an even lower-fat version, omit the pecans.

Calories—40; Saturated fat—0 g.; Total fat—1 g.; Carbohydrates—7 g.; Cholesterol—0 mg.; Sodium—0 mg.

ALGERIAN CHAROSET

PAREVE

From the Algerian-French family of my sister-in-law, Joelle.
It is their custom to save their pomegranates from Rosh Hashanah
and grind it into the Pesach charoset. The thousands of tiny seeds
in the pomegranate are considered a symbol of fertility.

½ cup pecans or walnuts
½ lb. dates
½ cup dried figs

2 small apples
¼ tsp. ginger
2 tbsp. sweet red wine

In a food processor puree the nuts and fruits. Stir in the ginger and wine. Makes approximately 2 cups.

Per 1-tbsp. serving: Calories—89; Saturated fat—0 g.; Total fat—1 g.; Carbohydrates—16 g.; Cholesterol—0 mg.; Sodium—1 mg.

Breakfast

FORTY YEARS IN THE DESERT TRAIL MIX

PAREVE

Since this takes some time, it's a good idea to make this soon after you clean your kitchen of the chometz. Try it! It's bound to be a hit!

7 matzahs
½ cup shredded coconut
½ cup carrots, shredded
3 small apples, unpeeled, cored, quartered, and thinly sliced crosswise
1½ tsp. cinnamon

¾ cup warm orange juice
1 tbsp. oil
¼ cup honey
4 tbsp. apple juice concentrate
½ cup sliced almonds
8 oz. dried mixed fruits, cut into bite-sized pieces

Preheat oven to 250 degrees.

In a large bowl, break up the matzahs into small pieces slightly larger than farfel (about ½ inch). Combine matzah with the coconut, carrots, apples, and cinnamon.

In a small bowl, combine the warm orange juice, oil, honey, and apple juice concentrate. Stir until the honey blends in. Drizzle over the matzah mixture and mix well. Let the mixture sit 2-3 minutes to absorb some of the liquid, then mix again.

Spread the mixture onto two nonstick baking sheets and bake for two hours, stirring mixture every 30 minutes. (Mixture will still be very moist after the first 30 minutes.) Add the almonds during the last 20 minutes. Then cool, transfer to a large bowl, and mix in the fruit. Makes about 9 cups.

Note: Store in a plastic covered container. Great as a cereal with milk or with yogurt or as a nosh by itself.

Calories—96; Saturated fat—1 g.; Total fat—3 g.; Carbohydrates—16 g.; Cholesterol—0 mg.; Sodium—9 mg.

SKILLET MATZAH BREI

PAREVE

*Wow! My kids say they actually like this version better—
without all the egg yolks and oil.*

Cooking spray
2 tsp. oil
4 matzahs
4 egg whites

½ tsp. onion powder, or to taste
¼ tsp. salt
⅛ tsp. black pepper

Coat a large nonstick skillet or griddle with cooking spray and add ½ teaspoon of the oil. Heat the skillet over medium-high heat until very hot. Meanwhile, moisten the matzah with cold water and crumble into a bowl. Add the egg whites and seasonings.

Spoon half the mixture into the hot skillet or griddle as one large pancake and brown. With a wide spatula, lift the matzah and add another ½ teaspoon of oil. Turn to brown the other side. Repeat procedure with remaining mixture and oil. Serves 4.

Calories—157; Saturated fat—0 g.; Total fat—2 g.; Carbohydrates—27 g.; Cholesterol—0 mg.; Sodium—202 mg.

PASSOVER LITE

SWEET ORANGE MATZAH BREI

This has the sweet essence of orange.
Serve it with orange marmalade for a real treat.

4 matzahs
½-⅔ cup orange juice
¼ cup Passover egg substitute
2 egg whites
Finely grated peel of 1 orange (1 tbsp.)

1½ tsp. sugar
Cooking spray
2 tsp. oil
Orange wedges and orange marmalade for garnish

Break up the matzahs and mix with the orange juice. (Add a little more than ½ cup if a softer matzah brei is preferred.) Let stand 1-2 minutes. Mix in the egg substitute, egg whites, orange peel, and sugar.

Spray a nonstick skillet with the cooking spray. Heat ½ teaspoon of the oil over medium-high heat. Spoon half of the mixture into the hot skillet as one large pancake and brown. With a wide spatula, lift the matzah and add another ½ teaspoon of oil. Turn to brown the other side. Repeat procedure with remaining mixture and oil. Serves 4.

Calories—177; Saturated fat—0 g.; Total fat—2 g.; Carbohydrates—33 g.; Cholesterol—6 mg.; Sodium—51 mg.

APPLE MATZAH BREI

You'll wonder where this dish has been all your life.

2 cups farfel
½ cup apple juice
Cooking spray
1 tsp. oil

2 egg whites
2-3 tbsp. applesauce
½ tsp. cinnamon
½ tsp. sugar

In a bowl, combine the farfel and apple juice. Coat a griddle with the cooking spray and add ½ teaspoon of the oil. Heat until the griddle is very hot. Mix in the egg whites, applesauce, cinnamon, and sugar. Spoon mixture onto the hot griddle as 6 pancakes and brown. With a wide spatula, lift the matzah and add the remaining oil. Turn to brown the other side. Serve with Apple Syrup, honey, jam, or applesauce. Makes 6 pancakes.

Calories—77; Saturated fat—0 g.; Total fat—1 g.; Carbohydrates—15 g.; Cholesterol—0 mg.; Sodium—19 mg.

APPLE SYRUP

1 cup apple juice
1 tbsp. honey

2 tsp. potato starch
Dash cinnamon

Combine all of the ingredients in a small saucepan over medium heat and stir until the mixture thickens. Serve warm. Serves 6.

Per 2-tbsp. serving: Calories—27; Saturated fat—0 g.; Total fat—0 g.; Carbohydrates—7 g.; Cholesterol—0 mg.; Sodium—1 mg.

CLASSIC CHEESE BLINTZES (LOW-CAL STYLE)

My grandma, Mollie Ashkanazi, was known for her blintzes. I still remember as a young girl when she took a Sunday afternoon and demonstrated her art.

BLINTZ BATTER

4 egg whites
1 cup skim milk
1/3 cup cake meal

1/4 cup potato starch
Cooking spray

In a medium bowl, beat the batter ingredients (all except the cooking spray) with an electric mixer until the batter is smooth and frothy.

If you are going to use this within 15 minutes, store it in the freezer while preparing the filling. Otherwise, cover and refrigerate until needed. Remember to beat the batter until frothy again just before using.

Coat a 7-inch nonstick saute pan with the cooking spray and heat over medium heat until it is hot. Stir the blintz batter, then pour a scant 1/4 cup of batter at a time into the pan, tipping the pan until the batter spreads. Cook until the top appears dry. Turn each blintz on to a platter or waxed paper cooked side up. Repeat procedure until the batter is used up; it will yield about 10 blintzes.

FILLING

¾ cup lowfat low-sodium cottage cheese

¾ cup lowfat Ricotta or dry cottage cheese

1 tbsp. sugar or apple juice concentrate

¼ tsp. cinnamon, or to taste

Cooking spray

2 tsp. oil

1 cup strawberries, quartered, for garnish

⅓ cup nonfat plain yogurt for garnish

To prepare the filling, in a small bowl, combine the cottage cheese, Ricotta, sugar, and cinnamon and mix with an electric beater until smooth and creamy.

For each blintz, spoon about 1 heaping tablespoonful of the cheese filling on the end nearest you, roll over once, fold sides in towards the middle, and complete the roll.

To brown your blintzes, spray a saute pan with more cooking spray, and use 1 teaspoon of the oil for each batch. Heat the saute pan over medium heat, then lightly brown both sides. Garnish the blintzes with the strawberries and yogurt. Makes 10 blintzes.

Variation: For Blueberry Blintzes, combine 1 cup blueberries with some Sugarless Blueberry Jam to taste.

Calories—49; Saturated fat—0 g.; Total fat—1 g.; Carbohydrates—5 g.; Cholesterol—3 mg.; Sodium—82 mg.

MOCK BLINTZ SOUFFLE

DAIRY

*If you don't want the work of Classic Cheese Blintzes
but do want the flavor, this is the simpler version.*

Cooking spray
½ lb. dry cottage cheese
½ lb. lowfat Ricotta cheese
½ cup orange juice
¼ cup sugar

2 tsp. cinnamon
3 whole matzahs
2 cups nonfat plain yogurt
8 egg whites
1½ tsp. vanilla

Preheat the oven to 350 degrees.

Coat bottom and sides of a 9-by-9-inch baking pan with cooking spray. In a food processor, process the cheeses, ¼ cup of the orange juice, 1 tablespoon of the sugar, and 1 teaspoon of the cinnamon.

Dip the whole matzahs in cold water for 1 minute to soften but not to soak and drain. Layer 1 matzah in the pan and spread with half of the cheese mixture (beyond the edges is OK). Layer the second matzah and spread with the remaining cheese mixture. Layer the third matzah.

In a bowl, blend together the yogurt, egg whites, vanilla and remaining orange juice, cinnamon, and sugar. Pour over the matzahs. Bake in the preheated oven for 50-60 minutes or until set. Let sit 10 minutes before serving. Serves 6.

Serving suggestion: Serve with Strawberry Sauce.

Calories—234; Saturated fat—0 g.; Total fat—0 g.; Carbohydrates—35 g.; Cholesterol—8 mg.; Sodium—157 mg.

PEACHES 'N' CREAM SMOOTHIE

DAIRY

1 cup fresh or canned peaches
½ cup skim milk
½ cup nonfat plain yogurt
½ tsp. vanilla

⅓ cup ice cubes
⅛ tsp. ginger
⅛ tsp. nutmeg

In a blender or food processor, puree the peaches with the milk. Add the remaining ingredients and blend until smooth. Serve immediately. Serves 2.

Calories—116; Saturated fat—0 g.; Total fat—0 g.; Carbohydrates—22 g.; Cholesterol—2 mg.; Sodium—61 mg.

MANGO SMOOTHIE

DAIRY

1 ripe mango, peeled and cut away from the pit
1 cup skim milk
½ cup pineapple juice

1 tbsp. lime juice
1 pitted date or ½ tbsp. honey
¼ cup ice

Puree all of the ingredients in a blender or food processor until smooth. Serve immediately. Serves 2.

Calories—167; Saturated fat—0 g.; Total fat—1 g.; Carbohydrates—35 g.; Cholesterol—2 mg.; Sodium—67 mg.

APRICOT BANANA SMOOTHIE

DAIRY/PAREVE

To make this pareve, substitute orange or apple juice for the milk.

½ cup water-packed apricots, drained, reserving liquid
1 large ripe banana
½ cup ice cubes

⅛ tsp. cinnamon
Dash nutmeg
1¼ cups skim milk

In a blender or food processor, puree all of the ingredients and add ¼ cup of the canned juice for sweetness. Serves 2.

Calories—136; Saturated fat—0 g.; Total fat—1 g.; Carbohydrates—27 g.; Cholesterol—2 mg.; Sodium—68 mg.

BANANA MUFFINS

PAREVE

1 banana mashed
2 tbsp. sugar
¾ cup orange juice
¼ cup Passover egg substitute
2 tsp. oil
Heaping ½ cup matzah meal

¼ cup potato starch
1 tsp. cinnamon
3 egg whites
1 tbsp. cinnamon and sugar mixture

Preheat the oven to 350 degrees.

Blend the banana, sugar, orange juice, egg substitute, and oil. In another bowl, combine the matzah meal, potato starch, and cinnamon. Add to the banana mixture. Mix well.

Beat the egg whites until stiff peaks form, but not dry. Fold in the egg whites until thoroughly blended. Divide evenly into a nonstick, large 12-muffin tin. Sprinkle the cinnamon-sugar mixture over the tops. Bake in the preheated oven for about 20-25 minutes or until the tops are lightly browned. Cool completely. Makes 12 muffins.

Calories—78; Saturated fat—0 g.; Total fat—1 g.; Carbohydrates—15 g.; Cholesterol—0 mg.; Sodium—23 mg.

APRICOT-PINEAPPLE "JAM"

PAREVE

A perfect topping on matzah or Banana Muffins. Or the kids might be tempted to just lick it right off the spoon.

8 oz. dried apricots
2 cups pineapple juice
3 dates

8 oz. unsweetened crushed pineapple, drained

In a small bowl, soak the apricots in the pineapple juice overnight.

The next day, transfer to a saucepan and add the crushed pineapple and dates for sweetness. Bring to a boil, reduce heat to low, and simmer about 30 minutes or until most of the liquid is absorbed.

In a food processor or blender, puree the apricot mixture. Store in a covered container and refrigerate. Makes approximately 2 cups.

Per 1-tbsp. serving: Calories—52; Saturated fat—0 g.; Total fat—0 g.; Carbohydrates—12 g.; Cholesterol—0 mg.; Sodium—2 mg.

SUGARLESS BLUEBERRY JAM

PAREVE

This is delicious if you love blueberries.

2 heaping cups frozen blueberries
½ cup raisins
½ tsp. cinnamon

1 tsp. potato starch
4 tbsp. apple juice concentrate
⅓ cup water

In a saucepan, combine the blueberries, raisins, and cinnamon. Dissolve the potato starch in the apple juice concentrate and water. Stir into the blueberry mixture. Cook over medium-high heat until the mixture comes to a boil. Reduce the heat to low and simmer, partly covered, for 30 minutes. Mash or puree in blender or food processor to the desired consistency. Spoon into a container and refrigerate. Makes approximately 2⅓ cups.

Per 1-tbsp. serving: Calories—20; Saturated fat—0 g.; Total fat—0 g.; Carbohydrates—5 g.; Cholesterol—0 mg.; Sodium—1 mg.

PASSOVER ROLLS

PAREVE

*These are lighter Passover rolls than you're used to.
They work great for sandwich fillings or you can enjoy them
for breakfast with a little jam or lowfat cheese.*

¾ cup matzah meal
¼ cup potato starch
¼ tsp. salt
¼ tsp. onion powder (optional if
   not for breakfast)

Dash white pepper
1 cup water
1 tbsp. oil
4 egg whites
Cooking spray

Preheat the oven to 375 degrees.

In a medium bowl, combine the dry ingredients.

In a saucepan, bring the water and oil to a boil. Mix into the matzah meal mixture. Add the egg whites, one at a time, and beat thoroughly after each one. (Totally, you should beat the mixture about 2 minutes.) Set aside for 10 minutes. Generously coat a foil-covered cookie sheet with cooking spray and drop the batter by tablespoonfuls. Bake for 35-40 minutes or until golden brown. Pull up from foil immediately. Makes 10 rolls.

Variation: Use 6 egg whites for a flatter roll with a smoother texture. Combine two to make a sandwich.

Calories—60; Saturated fat—0 g.; Total fat—0 g.; Carbohydrates—12 g.; Cholesterol—0 mg.; Sodium—141 mg.

MINIATURE PASSOVER BAGELS

PAREVE

1½ cups matzah meal
¼ tsp. salt
1 tbsp. sugar
1 cup water

1 tbsp. oil
½ cup Passover egg substitute
Cooking spray

Preheat the oven to 375 degrees.

In a medium bowl, combine the matzah meal, salt, and sugar.

In a saucepan, bring the water and oil to a boil. Add to the matzah meal mixture. With a mixer, blend in the egg substitute for about 2 minutes.

Coat a nonstick baking sheet with the cooking spray and drop the batter by table-spoonfuls. Make a hole in the center of each. Bake for 30 minutes or until golden brown. Remove immediately from the baking sheet to cool. Makes 1 dozen.

Calories—81; Saturated fat—0 g.; Total fat—1 g.; Carbohydrates—15 g.; Cholesterol—0 mg.; Sodium—65 mg.

Salads,
Dressings,
and Dips

STEAMED ARTICHOKES

Artichokes are delicious and bountifully available in the spring, right around Passover. This is the time to take advantage of their availability. They can be used as an appetizer with a dip from this book or a low-calorie bottled salad dressing. They can also be stuffed and served as a main course.

5-6 artichokes
2 cups water

1 lemon, sliced in half
2 garlic cloves

Remove stems from the artichokes. Trim the tips of leaves. Slice ¼ inch of the top off of each artichoke. Steam the artichokes with the remaining ingredients for 35-40 minutes or until the leaves can be easily pulled from the stem. Drain and serve with a dip or dressing or use in Artichokes with Matzah Stuffing. Serves 4-6.

Calories—85; Saturated fat—0 g.; Total fat—0 g.; Carbohydrates—16 g.; Cholesterol—0 mg.; Sodium—132 mg.

JERUSALEM PLATTER

PAREVE

This is definitely a showy platter. It is a beautiful and tasty appetizer for a seder. By the way, the artichoke marinade is also good on a lettuce salad.

ARTICHOKE MARINADE

¼ cup lemon juice
¼ cup dry red wine vinegar
2 tsp. minced fresh parsley

2 garlic cloves, minced
2 tsp. oil
Black pepper to taste

Mix the ingredients together and hold on the side.

4 artichokes
1 eggplant
½ lb. mushrooms, sliced
Artichoke leaves

2 cups cherry tomatoes, sliced in half
2 lemons, cut into wedges
Parsley sprigs

Slice the artichokes in half and steam until tender, about 40 minutes.

Meanwhile, slice the eggplant into 1-inch chunks and steam until fork-tender (about 10 minutes). During the last 2-3 minutes, add the sliced mushrooms. Drain and transfer to a bowl.

Scrape out the artichoke thistles and cut the bottom away from the leaves, reserving the leaves. Cut the artichoke bottoms into bite-sized pieces and mix with the eggplant and mushrooms. Add the cherry tomatoes. Pour the marinade over the vegetables. Chill at least 1 hour.

Next Year in Jerusalem

To serve, drain any marinade. Scoop the artichoke mixture onto a platter. Line the edges of the platter with enough artichoke leaves in layers to fan around the vegetables. Place lemon wedges evenly around the platter. Spread parsley sprigs around and on top for color. Serves 6-8.

Serving suggestion: Serve this as a first course with Matzah Snack Crackers.

Calories—89; Saturated fat—0 g.; Total fat—1 g.; Carbohydrates—14 mg.; Cholesterol—0 mg.; Sodium—72 mg.

MEDITERRANEAN EGGPLANT SALAD

PAREVE

Many Israeli eggplant salads contain a lot of oil. This is a slimmed-down version of one of the many types of eggplant salads.

1 large eggplant
1 large tomato, diced
¼ cup scallions, green part only
2 garlic cloves, minced

3½ tbsp. lemon juice
½ tsp. black pepper
2 tbsp. fresh parsley, snipped

Preheat the oven to 400 degrees.

Pierce the eggplant with a fork and bake until it is tender (about 40 minutes). Cool, peel, and mash the eggplant pulp. Drain well. In a bowl, mix the remaining ingredients together (including the eggplant pulp). Chill. Serve with Matzah Snack Crackers. Makes approximately 2 cups.

Serving suggestion: To serve as an appetizer, line a round platter or individual plates with lettuce leaves and mound on the salad. Top with parsley sprigs. Surround the mound with thin wedges of a tomato. Pass around the Matzah Snack Crackers. Serves 6.

Calories—30; Saturated fat—0 g.; Total fat—0 g.; Carbohydrates—6 g.; Cholesterol—6 g.; Sodium—10 mg.

SIX-CUP VEGETABLE SALAD

MEAT/PAREVE

Just as the vegetable combinations are variable, marinades are also interchangeable. The Artichoke Marinade from the Jerusalem Platter could also be used in this salad.

6 cups (about 1½ lb.) of any combination of the following vegetables: broccoli florets, cauliflower florets, sliced zucchini or yellow squash, sliced asparagus, whole baby carrots
Vegetable Marinade

Bring a pot with 2 inches of water to a boil. Steam each vegetable separately 1-2 minutes until cooked to desired tenderness. In a colander, hold the vegetables under very cold water to cool them. Transfer the vegetables to a salad bowl and add the Vegetable Marinade. Serves 6.

VEGETABLE MARINADE

½ cup chicken broth or vegetable stock
3 tbsp. red wine vinegar
2 scallions, chopped

1 tbsp. fresh parsley, chopped
1 tbsp. fresh cilantro or fresh dill, chopped

Puree all of the ingredients in a food processor. Pour over the vegetables and chill.

Calories—32; Saturated fat—0 g.; Total fat—0 g.; Carbohydrates—1 g.; Cholesterol—0 mg.; Sodium—263 mg.

ASPARAGUS-ARTICHOKE SALAD

PAREVE

½ lb. asparagus, tough ends
  snapped off, steamed until tender
½ lb. baby fresh artichokes,
  trimmed and steamed until
  tender
½ red bell pepper, thinly sliced
½ orange or yellow bell pepper,
  thinly sliced

¼ cup lemon juice
2 tsp. oil
2 tbsp. minced fresh dill, or to
  taste
⅛ tsp. black pepper, or to taste
4 cups mixed salad greens, such
  as romaine lettuce, Belgian
  endive, and spinach

Immerse the steamed asparagus and artichokes in a bowl of ice-cold water to stop the cooking process. Slice the asparagus stalks into 2-inch pieces, and the artichokes into halves. In a bowl, combine the asparagus, artichokes, and bell peppers.

In a small bowl or measuring cup, combine the lemon juice, oil, dill, and black pepper. Toss with the vegetable mixture. Chill. Serve over bed of salad greens on each individual salad plate. Serves 4.

Variation: This salad can be tossed with any vinaigrette in this chapter.

Calories—87; Saturated fat—0 g.; Total fat—3 g.; Carbohydrates—12 g.; Cholesterol—0 mg.; Sodium—70 mg.

PICKLED VEGETABLES

PAREVE

This might be good to make ahead, as soon as your kitchen is ready for Passover, because the longer the vegetables pickle, the better they taste.

3 cucumbers, cut into spears
4 carrots, cut into julienne slices
7 sprigs fresh dill

½ small onion, sliced and
  separated into rings

In a 2½- to 3-quart container, mix the vegetables and dill, leaving several sprigs on top.

PICKLE JUICE

1 cup water
1 cup vinegar
1 tbsp. kosher salt (optional)

3 cloves garlic, peeled
8 peppercorns

In a saucepan, combine the water and vinegar. Bring to a boil. Remove from the heat and dissolve the salt into the vinegar mixture. Add the garlic cloves and peppercorns. Pour over the vegetables. Cover tightly and refrigerate for at least 2 days. Serves 8.

Variation: You may substitute other veggies such as turnips, celeriac, red peppers, and cauliflower as some interesting choices to fill up a 2½- to 3-quart container.

Calories—23; Saturated fat—0 g.; Total fat—0 g.; Carbohydrates—5 g.; Cholesterol—0 mg.; Sodium—6 mg.

GARDEN COTTAGE CHEESE SALAD

DAIRY

Some like it hot. Some do not. This is a personal salad.
Play with the ingredients to suit your taste.

2 cups lowfat, low-sodium cottage cheese
½ cup tomato, seeded and finely diced
½ cup celery, finely diced
½ cup green pepper, finely diced, or ½ cup carrot, shredded

¼ tsp. celery seed
1 tbsp. white horseradish, or to taste
¼ tsp. black pepper, or to taste
⅛ tsp. cayenne pepper (optional)
Lettuce leaves

Combine all of the ingredients, except the lettuce leaves, in a medium bowl. Adjust the seasonings to taste.

Arrange the lettuce on individual plates and spoon the cottage cheese salad on top. Serves 4.

Calories—93; Saturated fat—1 g.; Total fat—1 g.; Carbohydrates—6 g.; Cholesterol—5 mg.; Sodium—129 mg.

POTATO SALAD

MEAT/PAREVE

A nice balance of flavors. You won't miss the mayonnaise.

2 lb. small red potatoes
½ cup celery, finely chopped
2 tsp. oil
¼ cup balsamic or white wine vinegar

¼ cup chicken or vegetable stock
1 tbsp. fresh parsley, minced
1 tbsp. fresh chives, minced
Black pepper to taste

Boil the potatoes until tender. While they are still warm, slice the potatoes into ½-inch slices. Transfer to a salad bowl and add the celery.

In a small saucepan, heat together the remaining ingredients until warmed through. Pour over the potato mixture and carefully toss to coat. May be served warm or cold. Serves 6.

Calories—182; Saturated fat—0 g.; Total fat—2 g.; Carbohydrates—38 g.; Cholesterol—0 mg.; Sodium—15 mg.

TOMATO GARLIC SALAD

PAREVE

6 tomatoes, sliced
6 chopped garlic cloves, or to taste
1 tbsp. fresh parsley, finely chopped

1 tbsp. oil
1 tbsp. red wine vinegar
½ tsp. black pepper, or to taste
1 tsp. fresh basil, chopped (optional)

Place the tomatoes in a serving dish. Mix the remaining ingredients, and pour over the tomatoes. Marinate for 30 minutes at room temperature, then chill. Serves 4.

Variation: Omit the garlic cloves and add 1-2 small red onions, sliced.

Calories—68; Saturated fat—2 g.; Total fat—2 g.; Carbohydrates—10 g.; Cholesterol—0 mg.; Sodium—19 mg.

CUCUMBER RADISH SALAD

PAREVE

This is a nice and light salad to put out for Shabbat lunch.

2 medium cucumbers peeled, thinly sliced
1 cup radishes, thinly sliced
¼ cup red onion, thinly sliced or chopped (optional)
2 tsp. oil

2 tbsp. white wine vinegar
2 tbsp. fresh parsley, finely chopped
2 tbsp. fresh chives, finely chopped
1 tbsp. fresh dill, finely chopped

In a salad bowl, combine the cucumber, radishes, and red onion.

In a small bowl, mix the remaining ingredients, and pour over the cucumber mixture. Marinate at room temperature for 30 minutes, then chill. Serves 4.

Calories—58; Saturated fat—0 g.; Total fat—3 g.; Carbohydrates—6 g.; Cholesterol—0 mg.; Sodium—15 mg.

RED CABBAGE SLAW

PAREVE

A take-off of the old red cabbage slaw. This is so mild in flavor even younger children really enjoy it, while getting the benefits of the vitamins and fiber.

Boiling water
3 cups red cabbage, shredded
1 large tart green apple, shredded
2 medium carrots, shredded
2 tbsp. red onion, finely chopped
¹⁄₃ cup apple juice

Juice of one lemon
1½ tbsp. cider vinegar
¹⁄₈ tsp. each salt and pepper
1 tsp. oil
2 tsp. cilantro leaves, finely chopped (optional)

Pour the boiling water over the cabbage to cover and let sit for 5 minutes to soften. Drain. Add the remaining ingredients and mix together. Chill and serve. Serves 4.

Calories—138; Saturated fat—0 g.; Total fat—2 g.; Carbohydrates—27 g.; Cholesterol—0 mg.; Sodium—290 mg.

CREAMY RUSSIAN SLAW

DAIRY

This recipe takes advantage of the low-fat, reduced-calorie products available. Personally, I find it helpful and convenient.

5 cups green cabbage, shredded
½ green or red bell pepper, cut into strips

2 carrots, shredded
4 radishes, thinly sliced

Combine all of the ingredients in a bowl. Prepare the dressing.

DRESSING

⅓ cup plain nonfat yogurt
½ cup Passover fat-free Russian salad dressing
1 tsp. sugar or sugar substitute

⅛ tsp. salt (optional)
1 tsp. poppy seeds (optional for Sephardim)

Combine the ingredients and toss into the slaw. Refrigerate. This tastes even better the next day. Serves 4-6.

Calories—55; Saturated fat—0 g.; Total fat—2 g.; Carbohydrates—8 g.; Cholesterol—1 mg.; Sodium—134 mg.

SHREDDED TRI-COLOR SALAD

PAREVE

The blend of the vegetables and fruit with the vinaigrette is deliciously refreshing. It's an upgraded slaw!

Lettuce or spinach leaves
1 Granny Smith apple, shredded
½ cup carrots, shredded
½ cup turnip or jicama, peeled and shredded

½ cup beets, peeled and shredded (or use shredded canned beets)
Zero-Fat Lemon Vinaigrette (recipe follows)

On a small platter covered with the lettuce or spinach leaves, spread the shredded apple across the leaves. On one end of shredded apples, neatly pile the carrots on top. Next to the carrots, pile the turnips; next to the turnips pile the beets.

Spoon Zero-Fat Lemon Vinaigrette over the vegetables or pass it around to individual plates. Serves 4.

Variation: The vegetables could all be mixed in a bowl with some of the vinaigrette blended in for flavor.

Calories—54; Saturated fat—0 g.; Total fat—0 g.; Carbohydrates—12 g.; Cholesterol—0 mg.; Sodium—11 mg.

ZERO-FAT LEMON VINAIGRETTE

PAREVE

¼ cup water
¼ cup lemon juice
½ cup red wine vinegar
¼ tsp. white pepper

½ small garlic clove, minced
1 tbsp. minced scallions
½ tsp. celery seed

In a jar, combine all of the ingredients and mix well. Serves 8.

Calories—10; Saturated fat—0 g.; Total fat—0 g.; Carbohydrates—1 g.; Cholesterol—0 mg.; Sodium—1 mg.

BROCCOLI DILL DIP

1 cup broccoli stems and florets,
  chopped and steamed until
  tender-crisp
½ cup lowfat cottage cheese
½ cup plain nonfat yogurt

2 garlic cloves, chopped
1 tbsp. fresh dill, chopped
1 tsp. dry chives
⅛ tsp. black pepper

Combine all of the ingredients in a food processor and blend until smooth. Seasonings may be adjusted. Chill before serving. Makes 1½ cups.

Calories—31; Saturated fat—0 g.; Total fat—0 g.; Carbohydrates—3 g.; Cholesterol—1 mg.; Sodium—96 mg.

TOMATO SALSA

PAREVE

*This is an easy recipe to double for the week and it's very versatile.
Try it, not only as a dip with veggies, but also use it as a topping for stuffed
baked potatoes, broiled fish, chicken or gefilte fish. I even made a soup
for it to go into. If you want a milder salsa, use Anaheim peppers.*

3 tomatoes, diced very small
½ small red onion, minced
2-3 jalapeno or serrano peppers, minced
1 large garlic clove, minced

4 tbsp. tomato paste
4 tbsp. water
2 tbsp. vinegar
2 sprigs cilantro, finely chopped

In a bowl or container, combine the tomato, onion, jalapeno peppers, and garlic. Blend the tomato paste, water, and vinegar together and mix into the salsa. Cover and refrigerate. Makes about 2½ cups.

Calories—23; Saturated fat—0 g.; Total fat—0 g.; Carbohydrates—4 mg.; Cholesterol—0 mg.; Sodium—8 mg.

MATZAH SNACK CRACKERS

PAREVE

Great with dips or by themselves—and only 10 calories each!

2 egg whites
2 tsp. garlic powder
2 tsp. onion powder
1 tsp. salt

½ tsp. paprika
1 8-oz. box Manischewitz Miniature Passover Matzah Crackers

Preheat the oven to 400 degrees.

In a small bowl, combine the egg whites, garlic and onion powders, salt, and paprika. Beat the egg white mixture until frothy.

Empty the crackers into a large bowl, and add the egg white mixture. Gently toss until the crackers are coated. Arrange the crackers in a single layer on a baking sheet. Bake on the bottom rack for 3 minutes. Turn the crackers over and bake for 1-2 minutes more. Cool completely. Makes approximately 94 crackers.

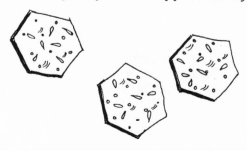

SALADS, DRESSINGS, AND DIPS

Serving suggestion: Make a big batch of these and use them with dips or Tomato Salsa.

For croutons: Break the crackers into bite-sized pieces and serve with Gazpacho or a salad.

Per cracker: Calories—10; Saturated fat—0 g.; Total fat—0 g.; Carbohydrates—2 mg.; Cholesterol—0 mg.; Sodium—0 mg., if adding salt—19 mg.

CELERY SEED TOMATO DRESSING

PAREVE

An excellent dressing for lettuce salads.

1 tsp. potato starch
1 cup low-sodium tomato sauce
4 tbsp. red wine vinegar
1 tsp. celery seed
½ tsp. paprika

¼ tsp. garlic powder
¼ tsp. onion powder
¼ tsp. black pepper
2 tbsp. apple juice concentrate

In a small saucepan combine the potato starch and tomato sauce over medium heat and stir constantly until the mixture just thickens. Remove from the heat and pour into a jar. Add the rest of the ingredients, shake, and chill. Makes approximately 1 cup.

Calories—27; Saturated fat—0 g.; Total fat—0 g.; Carbohydrates—4 g.; Cholesterol—0 mg.; Sodium—9 mg.

ZESTY TOMATO SALAD DRESSING

PAREVE

This is an old recipe that I played around with, getting the idea from a vegetarian restaurant that we like. It's a good, light dressing for vegetable and lettuce salads.

½ cup low-sodium tomato juice
¼ cup lemon juice
1 tbsp. oil
1 tsp. garlic, minced

½ tsp. onion powder
½ tsp. paprika
Black pepper to taste

Combine all of the ingredients in a jar and shake. Chill. Makes ⅔ cup.

Calories—54; Saturated fat—0 g.; Total fat—4 g.; Carbohydrates—5 g.; Cholesterol—0 mg.; Sodium—7 mg.

CREAMY FETA DRESSING

DAIRY

½ cup nonfat cottage cheese
1 cup nonfat plain yogurt
2 oz. feta cheese
1 cup fresh spinach, chopped

½ yellow or orange bell pepper, chopped
2 tsp scallions, chopped
1 tsp. dry dillweed

Combine all of the ingredients in a food processor. Process until smooth. Makes 1½ cups.

Calories—149; Saturated fat—1 g.; Total fat—2 g.; Carbohydrates—15 g.; Cholesterol—20 mg.; Sodium—282 mg.

Soups

CREAM OF MUSHROOM SOUP

This is definitely my family's favorite soup.

Cooking spray
2 leeks, white and light green
    parts only, rinsed and sliced
2 tbsp. celery, finely chopped
½ tsp. tumeric
½ tsp. coriander
½ tsp. cumin
⅛ tsp. black pepper
¼ tsp. salt

3 cups (8 oz.) white mushrooms,
    sliced
1 cup any fresh variety mush-
    room, such as shitake or por-
    tobello, sliced
3 cups skim milk
1 cup Vegetable Stock
2 tbsp. potato starch

Spray the bottom of a soup pot with the cooking spray. Saute the leeks and celery for about 2 minutes. Add the seasonings and mushrooms. Cook and stir for another 2-3 minutes to blend in seasonings.

Add the milk and ½ cup of the vegetable stock. Bring to a boil. Reduce heat and simmer for about 7 minutes.

Blend in the potato starch with the remaining ½ cup vegetable stock. Stir back into soup and continue stirring occasionally and simmering for another 7-10 minutes or until the soup heats through. Serves 4-5.

Variation: Omit the tumeric, coriander, and cumin. Replace with ¼ cup of white wine.

Calories—200; Saturated fat—0 g.; Total fat—1 g.; Carbohydrates—37 g.; Cholesterol—4 mg.; Sodium—604 mg.

CREAMY ASPARAGUS SOUP

DAIRY

Cooking spray
1 leek, white part only, rinsed
   and sliced
4 cups water
1 lb. asparagus, tough ends
   snapped off

1 small red potato
1 sprig fresh dill
½ cup skim milk
¼ cup nonfat dry milk
¼ tsp. salt, or to taste
⅛ tsp. black pepper

Spray the bottom of a soup pot with the cooking spray and saute the leek for 1 minute. Add the water, asparagus, potato, and dill. Cover and simmer for 15-20 minutes or until the potato is tender.

Transfer the vegetables in batches to a food processor or blender. Add the skim milk a little at a time to help puree the vegetables. In the last batch, include the non-fat dry milk. Return the vegetable mixture to the pot. Add salt and pepper and serve. Serves 4-5.

Calories—85; Saturated fat—0 g.; Total fat—0 g.; Carbohydrates—14 g.; Cholesterol—2 mg.; Sodium—176 mg.

VEGETABLE SOUP

MEAT/PAREVE

This is definitely a haimishe soup and a hearty meal.

Cooking spray
1 onion, finely diced
2 garlic cloves
3 cups Chicken or Vegetable
   Stock
4 medium carrots, sliced
1 lb. small red potatoes,
   scrubbed and cubed
28 oz. whole tomatoes, chopped

1 cup tomato puree
½ large green pepper, diced
2 small yellow squash, diced
2 parsley sprigs
1 tsp. basil
8 oz. spinach, rinsed, coarsely
   chopped
Juice of ½ lemon

Coat the bottom of soup pot with the cooking spray. Saute the onion and garlic until the onions are soft. Pour in the chicken broth and add the carrots and potatoes. Bring to a boil; reduce heat to medium. Cover and simmer for 20 minutes.

Add the whole tomatoes, tomato puree, green peppers, yellow squash, parsley, and basil; cover and simmer for 15 minutes or until the vegetables are tender. Add the spinach and lemon juice and simmer for another 5 minutes. Serves 6.

Calories—207; Saturated fat—0 g.; Total fat—1 g.; Carbohydrates—40 g.; Cholesterol—0 mg.; Sodium—261 mg.

TOMATO SALSA SOUP

PAREVE/DAIRY/MEAT

1½ cups water
1½ cups Tomato Salsa
1 cup low-sodium tomato juice
1 tsp. dry minced onion
½ tsp. basil
1 tsp. oregano or marjoram
⅛ tsp. black pepper

Dash garlic powder
1 16-oz. bag frozen mixed broccoli, cauliflower, carrots, thawed; or 4 cups fresh mixed vegetables
4 tsp. Parmesan cheese for garnish (optional)

Run water over the frozen vegetables to thaw them or steam the fresh vegetables until tender-crisp. Then combine all of the ingredients, except the Parmesan cheese, and simmer in a covered pot until heated through. Sprinkle the Parmesan cheese over individual bowls if desired. Serves 4.

Variation: For a hearty main dish, meat meal, leave out the Parmesan cheese and add these meatballs:

¾ lb. lean ground turkey
1 egg white
½ cup shredded potato
¼ tsp. oregano

⅛ tsp. black pepper
Cooking spray
½ cup water

In a small bowl, combine the ground turkey, egg white, potato, oregano, and pepper and form into small meatballs.

Coat a nonstick skillet with the cooking spray and brown the meatballs on all sides. Add the water and bring to a boil. Reduce the heat, cover, and simmer for 20 minutes. Transfer meatballs to the soup and heat through together.

Pareve version: Calories—96; Saturated fat—0 g.; Total fat—0 g.; Carbohydrates—19 g.; Cholesterol—0 mg.; Sodium—48 mg.

Dairy version: Calories—119; Saturated fat—1 g.; Total fat—2 g.; Carbohydrates—19 g.; Cholesterol—4 mg.; Sodium—141 mg.

Meat version: Calories—141; Saturated fat—0 g.; Total fat—1 g.; Carbohydrates—10 g.; Cholesterol—51 mg.; Sodium—81 mg.

RUSSIAN CABBAGE BORSCHT

MEAT

My grandma, Libbie Tecklin, made this soup a lot. She was always a no-nonsense person and her food was always simple but packed with flavor. Grandpa Jack liked this soup extra sweet and beefy but, for calories' sake, I reduced the sugar and meat. It still brings back memories.

BORSCHT

1 large onion, chopped
1 stalk celery, sliced
½ lb. lean chuck, cut into small chunks
4 cups canned low-sodium whole tomatoes

1 cup canned low-sodium tomato puree
½ medium head cabbage, slivered (3-4 cups)
6 cups water

In a large soup pot, combine borscht ingredients. Bring to a boil. Reduce heat, cover, and simmer about 1 hour.

SEASONINGS

½ tsp. citric acid (sour salt) or juice of half a lemon
¼ tsp. paprika

½ tsp. salt
¼ tsp. black pepper
1 tbsp. sugar, or to taste

Add seasonings and continue simmering, covered, over very low heat for another ½ hour. Adjust seasonings if needed for desired taste. Serves 4.

Variation: Add 3 potatoes, peeled and cut into chunks, to the soup for a heartier, but not fatter meal.

Calories—201; Saturated fat—2 g,; Total fat—6 g.; Carbohydrates—39 g.; Cholesterol—37 mg.; Sodium—453 mg.

MOM'S CHICKEN SOUP/CHICKEN BROTH

MEAT

Chicken soup's flavor is best when some of the skin is left on during cooking and removed after it sits overnight. Also, my mother, Bernice Ashkanazi, says the longer you simmer the soup, the more flavorful it will be. That's learning patience. For low-sodium diets substitute this chicken broth (with salt omitted) for recipes instead of the canned variety.

4 lb. chicken, skin a few large pieces
1 large onion, cut in half
4 qt. cold water
3 sprigs fresh dill or ½ tsp. dry dillweed

3-4 sprigs parsley
3 celery stalks and tops, chopped
3 large carrots, peeled and sliced
¾ tsp. salt, or to taste
Black pepper to taste

Rinse the chicken well and place in a soup pot. Add the onion and cover with cold water. Bring the water to a boil and skim as the froth forms at the top. Reduce the heat to medium-low. Cover partially and simmer for 1-1½ hours.

Tie together the parsley and dill sprigs with a string. Add this and the remaining ingredients to the soup. Continue to simmer, partially covered, on low for about 1½ hours.

Remove and discard the parsley-dill bundle.

Remove the chicken and place in a separate container to refrigerate. You may also want to remove some of the vegetables to make room for the matzah balls (although my mom never did).

Refrigerate the soup overnight and skim off the fat before reheating. Skin the chicken and serve on the side for a meal-in-one or save it for another recipe. Serves 6-8.

Variations: For Golden Chicken Soup, remove all of the vegetables and when ready to reheat, puree the cooked vegetables, return to the soup pot, and heat through.

For a Sephardic-style Chicken Soup with Lemon, add the juice of 2 lemons to the soup along with the parsley and dill sprigs.

Soup without chicken: Calories—81; Saturated fat—0 g.; Total fat—2 g.; Carbohydrates—7 g.; Cholesterol—0 mg; Sodium—247 mg.

Soup with chicken: Calories—262; Saturated fat—3 g.; Total fat—11 g.; Carbohydrates: 11g.; Cholesterol—8 mg.; Sodium—139 mg.

VEGETARIAN "CHICKEN" SOUP/VEGETABLE STOCK

PAREVE

*Include all the vegetables and matzah balls you want in this soup.
Who needs the chicken? You won't miss it. To use this as a basic
vegetable stock, strain the vegetables.*

9 cups water
2 onions, quartered
4 carrots, sliced
4 stalks celery, sliced, tops
  included
1/2 red bell pepper, chopped

3 large mushrooms, sliced
2 tbsp. dry soup greens
1/8-1/4 tsp. crushed peppercorns
1 1/2 tsp. salt
5 sprigs parsley
5 sprigs dill

In a soup pot combine the water, onions, carrots, celery, red bell pepper, mushrooms, soup greens, peppercorns, and salt. Bring to a boil. Reduce heat, cover, and simmer for 30 minutes.

Tie the parsley and dill sprigs together with a string and add to the soup. Cover and simmer for another 30 minutes.

Remove the parsley and dill. To make a broth for matzah ball soup, remove all of the vegetables, but leave some carrots in for color. Serves 8.

Calories—41; Saturated fat—0 g.; Total fat—0 g.; Carbohydrates—9 g.; Cholesterol—0 mg.; Sodium—89 mg.

THE LIGHTER MATZAH BALLS

PAREVE

You might want to double this recipe for a seder crowd.

4 egg whites
1 egg yolk
1 tsp. onion powder
1 tsp. salt (optional)

¼ tsp. black or white pepper
¾ cup matzah meal
2 tbsp. water

In a bowl, beat the egg whites until stiff but not dry. Lightly fold the egg yolk and seasonings into the beaten egg whites. Gently mix in the matzah meal and water until the dough is thoroughly blended. Chill for 30 minutes.

Bring a pot of water to a gentle boil. With damp hands, shape the dough into 1-inch balls. Drop them into the boiling water. Reduce the heat, cover, and simmer over medium-low heat for about 45 minutes. Transfer to lukewarm soup and heat through. Makes 12 balls.

Per matzah ball: Calories—40; Saturated fat—0 g.; Total fat—1 g.; Carbohydrates—7 g.; Cholesterol—17 mg.; Sodium—39 mg.

SOUP NOODLES

PAREVE

These are good in chicken soup.

1 cup Passover egg substitute
2 tbsp. potato starch

2 tbsp. water
Cooking spray

Thoroughly blend the first three ingredients.

Coat a nonstick skillet with the cooking spray and heat it over medium. Lightly fry the mixture on both sides. Turn out onto wax paper or a plate. Roll up and slice thinly. Serves 3-4.

Calories—47; Saturated fat—0 g.; Total fat—0 g.; Carbohydrates—6 g.; Cholesterol—0 mg.; Sodium—94 mg.

TOASTED MATZAH FARFEL

PAREVE

If you use ¼ cup for your soup, it should serve about 6.
Personally, this is so good to just nosh on it doesn't make it to my soup.
Maybe you should double the recipe.

3 cups matzah farfel	1 tsp. oil
¼ cup Passover egg substitute	1 tsp. onion powder
1 egg white	½ tsp. salt, or to taste

Preheat the oven to 350 degrees.
In a bowl, toss all of the ingredients until the farfel is coated.
Spread the farfel on a baking sheet and bake for 20-25 minutes. During this time, break it up and stir occasionally until lightly browned. Makes 12 ¼-cup servings.

Calories—65; Saturated fat—0 g.; Total fat—0 g.; Carbohydrates—13 g.; Cholesterol—0 mg.; Sodium—110 mg.

CHINESE HOT AND SOUR SOUP

MEAT/PAREVE

⅛ tsp. crushed red pepper	(if kosher-for-Passover bamboo
1 tsp. vinegar	shoots are not available, increase
1 boneless chicken breast half,	napa cabbage to 2 cups)
cut into narrow strips	4 tsp. potato starch
5¼ cups Chicken Stock	¼ cup water
3 tbsp. vinegar	¼ tsp. white pepper
½ tsp. salt (optional)	2 egg whites, lightly beaten
1 cup mushrooms, sliced	1 scallion, chopped, for garnish
1 cup napa cabbage, shredded	2 tsp. sesame seeds, toasted, for
1 8-oz. can bamboo shoots	garnish (optional for Sephardim)

In a small bowl combine the crushed red pepper and vinegar. Set aside.
In a nonstick skillet, cook the chicken strips in ¼ cup of the chicken broth until the chicken is no longer pink. Set aside.
In a 2-quart saucepan, combine the remaining broth, vinegar, and salt and bring to a boil. Reduce the heat and add the mushrooms and cabbage. Simmer covered for about 20 minutes. Add the chicken strips and bamboo shoots.

In a small bowl, combine the potato starch, water, and white pepper. Increase the heat to medium-high and add this mixture to the soup. Stir until it comes to a boil and slightly thickens.

Pour the lightly beaten egg whites in a slow, steady stream into the soup while stirring until the soup comes to a boil again and the egg whites turn white. (This should only take a minute or so.)

Add ¼ to 1 tsp. of the red pepper-vinegar mixture according to your taste.

Garnish individual soup bowls with the chopped scallion and toasted sesame seeds. Serves 4.

Variation: To make this vegetarian or pareve, use vegetable stock and add ½ cup each grated carrots, sliced mushrooms, and shredded cabbage.

Calories—115; Saturated fat—0 g.; Total fat—2 g.; Carbohydrates—8 g.; Cholesterol—17 mg.; Sodium—509 mg.

SWEET AND SOUR BEET BORSCHT

PAREVE/DAIRY

8 beets, tops trimmed
2 qt. water
3 tbsp. honey
⅓ cup lemon juice

⅓ cup orange juice concentrate, thawed
Nonfat plain yogurt (optional)

Scrub the beets well. Place the beets in a soup pot and add the water. Bring to a boil. Reduce heat, cover, and simmer for 30 minutes or until tender.

Remove beets and save the beet liquid. Cool, then peel and grate the beets. Return the beets and beet liquid to the pot, add the remaining ingredients, and gently simmer for another 15 minutes. Chill.

For a dairy meal, serve with a dollop of yogurt. Serves 8.

Calories—97; Saturated fat—0 g.; Total fat—0 g.; Carbohydrates—22 g.; Cholesterol—0 mg.; Sodium—72 mg.

GAZPACHO

PAREVE

This may be served with Matzah Snack Croutons or Toasted Matzah Farfel.
For a dairy meal, add a dollop of nonfat yogurt to individual bowls.

4 tomatoes
2 large cucumbers, peeled
½ medium green pepper, coarsely chopped
¼ cup red onion, chopped
2 cups low-sodium tomato juice

¼ cup white wine vinegar
1 tsp. oil
1 garlic clove
⅛ tsp. black pepper
⅛ tsp. cayenne pepper

Seed and coarsely chop 3 of the 4 tomatoes. Slice 1½ cucumbers in half. (The remaining tomato and cucumber will be used as garnish.)

Puree the 3 tomatoes and 1½ cucumbers, green pepper, and onion. Add the tomato juice, vinegar, oil, and seasonings. Transfer to a serving bowl. To serve, seed and chop the remaining tomato and cucumber and add to the bowl. Seasonings may be adjusted to taste. Serves 6.

Calories—60; Saturated fat—0 g.; Total fat—1 g.; Carbohydrates—11 g.; Cholesterol—0 mg.; Sodium—17 mg.

TROPICAL FRUIT SOUP

DAIRY

This is a favorite with the kids. The secret is the banana.

3 cups fresh strawberries, tops
removed
2 small mangoes or ½ canteloupe

1 banana
2 cups apple juice
1 cup nonfat plain yogurt

Blend all ingredients in a blender until smooth. Serves 4.

Variation: If available, try substituting one of the cups of apple juice with low-calorie cranberry juice, or substitute the strawberries with canned pitted sour cherries.

Calories—182; Saturated fat—0 g.; Total fat—1 g.; Carbohydrates—39 g.; Cholesterol—1 mg.; Sodium—48 mg.

Fish

LEAN GEFILTE FISH LOAF

PAREVE

This version of the old favorite saves you several steps!

2 lb. any whitefish fillets
2 medium onions, chopped
2 carrots, grated
½ cup matzah meal
¼ cup Passover egg substitute
2 egg whites

1 tsp. sugar
1 tsp. salt
¼ tsp. white pepper
½ cup cold water
Cooking spray
Cooked sliced carrots for garnish

Preheat the oven to 350 degrees.

In a food processor, grind the fish and onions.

In a mixing bowl, combine this mixture with the grated carrot, matzah meal, egg substitute, egg whites, sugar, salt, pepper, and cold water.

Place the mixture in a loaf pan that has been coated with the cooking spray. Bake in the preheated oven for 1 hour. Do not let it brown. Cool in the pan. Turn it out, cover tightly, and refrigerate.

Slice and serve on a lettuce leaf with Horseradish (Chraine). Garnish with cooked sliced carrots. Serves 10.

Calories—167; Saturated fat—0 g.; Total fat—2 g.; Carbohydrates—14 g.; Cholesterol—64 mg.; Sodium—125 mg.

BOULETTE DE POISSON

A Sephardic Pesach first course
from my Algerian-French sister-in-law Joelle Hankin

1 lb. whitefish fillet, such as cod
  or pollack
⅓ cup matzah meal
2 garlic cloves
2 scallions
¼ cup parsley, chopped
1 egg white

⅓ cup cake meal
Cooking spray
2 tsp. oil
8 oz. can low-sodium tomato
  puree
¼ cup water
3 oz. capers, drained, rinsed

Combine the fish, matzah meal, garlic, scallions, parsley, and egg white in a food processor and process until the ingredients are smooth.

With wet hands, form the fish into patties. Coat each patty on both sides with the cake meal.

Coat a large nonstick frying pan with the cooking spray. Heat over medium-high heat until very hot. Add the oil. Brown the patties on both sides. Remove and set aside.

In the same skillet, reduce the heat to medium, add the tomato puree, water, and capers. Simmer for 10 minutes.

Return the patties to the skillet to heat through both the patties and the sauce. Serves 4.

Calories—190; Saturated fat—0 g.; Total fat—4 g.; Carbohydrates—16 g.; Cholesterol—49 mg.; Sodium—264 mg.

SMOKED WHITEFISH FRITTADA

DAIRY

*This is makes a delicious brunch dish, especially when paired up
with Fresh Fruit Salad. Some of the veggies that are good to use in this dish
are carrots, broccoli, red pepper, mushrooms, and celery.*

8 oz. smoked whitefish, skinned
and flaked
3 cups fresh or frozen mixed
vegetables, steamed
6 large egg whites
1 scallion

1 tbsp. lemon juice
¼ tsp. dill
1 garlic clove, minced
Cooking spray
2 oz. lowfat yellow cheese
Lemon slices for garnish

Preheat the oven to 350 degrees.

Combine the first 7 ingredients and turn into a baking dish coated with the cooking spray. Bake in the preheated oven for 15 minutes.

Arrange the cheese across the top and continue to bake for 15 minutes or until the eggs are set and the cheese melts. Garnish with the lemon slices. Serves 4.

*Calories—193; Saturated fat—1 g.; Total fat—3 g.; Carbohydrates—15 g.;
Cholesterol—26 mg.; Sodium—1129 mg.*

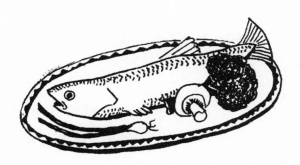

SEASONED FISH IN WINE SAUCE

PAREVE

1 tsp. basil
1½ tsp. thyme
½ tsp. black pepper
Dash cayenne pepper

1½ lb. halibut steaks, or other
   firm whitefish
Cooking spray
2 tsp. oil
Lemon slices for garnish

Combine seasonings and sprinkle onto fish. Coat a nonstick skillet with the cooking spray. Over medium heat, add the oil. When the skillet is hot, fry the fish on each side for about 4-5 minutes or until the fish is opaque throughout. Prepare the sauce.

SAUCE

⅔ cup dry white wine
2 garlic cloves, minced

3 tbsp. lemon juice
¾ tsp. potato starch

In a small saucepan, heat the ingredients together over medium heat until slightly thickened. Serve the fish on a platter with the sauce spooned over the top. Garnish with the lemon slices. Serves 4.

Calories—236; Saturated fat—1 g.; Total fat—6 g.; Carbohydrates—3 g.; Cholesterol—54 mg.; Sodium—95 mg.

SPICY SESAME FISH

PAREVE

¼ cup matzah meal
1 tbsp. sesame seeds
1 tsp. cumin
1 tsp. onion powder
½ tsp. garlic powder
½ tsp. paprika
⅛-¼ tsp. cayenne pepper

1 egg white mixed with 1 tbsp.
   water
1½ lb. whitefish fillets, such as
   cod, pike, or pollock
Cooking spray
2 tsp. oil

Combine the matzah meal, sesame seeds, and seasonings on a plate. In another shallow dish or plate combine the egg white and water. Dip the fish in the egg white mixture, then in the coating mixture.

Coat a nonstick skillet with the cooking spray and add 1 teaspoon of the oil.

Heat the skillet to medium-high. When the skillet is hot, add the fish and fry for 5 minutes on one side, adding the remaining oil, and fry for 5 minutes on the other side. Serves 4.

Variation: Omit the sesame seeds and cumin and increase the paprika to 1½ teaspoons.

Calories—205; Saturated fat—1 g.; Total fat—5 g.; Carbohydrates—6 g.; Cholesterol—73 mg.; Sodium—94 mg.

PARMESAN FILLETS

DAIRY

1½ lb. whitefish fillets, such as flounder or cod
Juice of ½ lemon
Lemon pepper to taste
½ cup matzah meal

3 tbsp. Parmesan cheese
2 egg whites, beaten with 2 tbsp. water
Cooking spray
2 tsp. oil

Rinse and pat the fish dry with a paper towel.

Squeeze the lemon juice over the fish and sprinkle lightly with the lemon pepper. Combine the matzah meal and Parmesan cheese. Dip the fish in the egg white mixture, then coat both sides in the matzah meal mixture.

Coat a nonstick skillet with the cooking spray. Over medium heat, add 1 teaspoon of the oil. When the skillet is hot, fry the fish for 4-5 minutes on one side. Turn the fish over, add the remaining oil, and continue to fry for 4-5 minutes, or until fish is lightly browned and opaque throughout. Serves 4.

Calories—258; Saturated fat—1 g.; Total fat—6 g.; Carbohydrates—15 g.; Cholesterol—85 mg.; Sodium—346 mg.

FISH IN TANGY TOMATO SAUCE

PAREVE

Cooking spray
1-1½ lb. whitefish fillets, such as
   pollock, sole, or cod
Black pepper
1 medium onion, finely chopped

2 tbsp. cider vinegar
1 tbsp. apple juice concentrate
1 cup tomato puree
½ tsp. paprika
Dash cayenne pepper, or to taste

Preheat the oven to 350 degrees.

Spray a shallow baking dish with the cooking spray. Arrange the fish in a single layer. Sprinkle the fish with black pepper.

Spray a nonstick saute pan with the cooking spray and lightly brown the onions. Mix in the remaining ingredients and pour over the fish. Bake uncovered in the preheated oven for 25 minutes, or until fish is opaque throughout. Serves 4.

Calories—152; Saturated fat—0 g.; Total fat—2 g.; Carbohydrates—11 g.; Cholesterol—44 mg.; Sodium—90 mg.

CHILI-STUFFED SALMON POTATOES

DAIRY

Try serving this with Cucumber Radish Salad.

4 medium potatoes, baked
2 Anaheim chili peppers
¼ cup skim milk
¼ cup nonfat plain yogurt
1 scallion, finely chopped

12 oz. canned salmon (remove
   bones and skin)
⅛ tsp. cayenne pepper
¼ cup lowfat Muenster (or other
   white) cheese, shredded (optional)

Preheat the oven to 350 degrees.

While the potatoes are baking, roast the chili peppers (see the Roasted Peppers recipe) and finely chop them.

Scoop the pulp out of the potatoes, but leave a ¼-inch lining around the shells for support. Mash the potatoes with the milk and yogurt. If mixture is too dry, add more milk and yogurt to reach the desired consistency.

Mix in the chili peppers, salmon, scallion, and cayenne pepper. Spoon the mixture back into the shells. Sprinkle on the cheese and bake at 350 degrees until heated through. Serves 4.

Calories—359; Saturated fat—1 g.; Total fat—5 g.; Carbohydrates—55 g.; Cholesterol—47 mg.; Sodium—507 mg.

DILLED SALMON IN POTATOES

DAIRY

*This is a quick and simple meal in one. A light salad
with any of the fat-free dressings is a good accompaniment.*

4 medium potatoes, baked
¼ cup skim milk
¼ cup nonfat plain yogurt
12 oz. fresh or canned salmon,
  bones and skin removed,
  drained

2 tbsp. dry chives
1 tbsp. fresh dill, finely chopped
2 tbsp. lemon juice
½ cup lowfat cheese, shredded

Preheat the oven to 350 degrees.

Scoop the pulp out of the potato, but leave a ¼-inch lining around the shell for support. Add the milk and yogurt and mash into the potatoes. Stir and mash in the salmon. If the mixture is too dry, add more milk and yogurt to reach the desired consistency.

Mix in the seasonings and lemon juice. (Seasonings and lemon juice may also be adjusted according to the size of the potato and taste.)

Spoon back into the shells and sprinkle the cheese on top. Bake in the preheated oven until heated through and the cheese melts. Serves 4.

Calories—400; Saturated fat—3 g.; Total fat—6 g.; Carbohydrates—54 g.; Cholesterol—56 mg.; Sodium—583 mg.

TUNA PATTIES

PAREVE

2 cans (6½ oz.) tuna, water-
  packed, drained
½ cup onions, finely chopped
½ cups carrots, shredded
1 cup celery, sliced
¼ tsp. pepper
¼ cup fresh parsley, finely

chopped, or 2 tbsp. dry parsley flakes
2 tsp. horseradish
2 egg whites
½ cup matzah meal
2 tsp. oil

In a bowl, combine all of the ingredients, except the oil.

In a nonstick skillet, heat the oil. Form the tuna mixture into patties and fry at medium-high heat on both sides until brown. Serve immediately. Serves 4.

Variation: Substitute salmon for the tuna.

Calories—217; Saturated fat—0 g.; Total fat—3 g.; Carbohydrates—18 g.; Cholesterol—15 mg.; Sodium—364 mg.

POACHED SALMON IN ORANGE VINAIGRETTE

PAREVE

2½ cups water
1 onion, sliced
4 salmon fillets (5 oz. each)
3 tbsp. orange juice concentrate
8 peppercorns

1 bay leaf
1 tsp. fresh dill or ¼ tsp. dry
  dillweed
⅓ cup vinegar

Add the water and sliced onion to a pan. Bring to a boil and cook the onion for 5 minutes.

Add the salmon, orange juice concentrate, peppercorns, bay leaf, and dill. Reduce to a simmer, cover, and simmer for 20 minutes. Add the vinegar and continue to simmer 10 minutes more.

Transfer the fish to a shallow dish and pour the sauce over the fish. Cover and chill before serving. Serves 4.

Calories—247; Saturated fat—2 g.; Total fat—7 g.; Carbohydrates—12 g.; Cholesterol—54 mg.; Sodium—57 mg.

TUNA IN A GREEN PEPPER BOAT

PAREVE

DRESSING

¼ cup low-sodium tomato juice
2 tbsp. lemon juice
¼ tsp. onion powder

¼ tsp. paprika
Pinch black pepper, or to taste

In a small bowl, combine the dressing ingredients.

TUNA SALAD

1 6½-oz. can water-packed tuna, drained
1 tbsp. green or red pepper, minced

1 small carrot, shredded
1 green pepper, halved lengthwise and seeded

In another bowl, combine the tuna, carrot, and minced pepper. Pour the dressing into the tuna salad and mix thoroughly. Fill the green pepper halves. Serves 1-2.

Variation: To add more kick to the salad, saute 1 tablespoon minced onion and ⅛ teaspoon minced garlic (about 1 small clove) in a nonstick skillet coated with cooking spray until the onions are lightly golden. Mix into the tuna salad.

Calories—149; Saturated fat—1 g.; Total fat—2 g.; Carbohydrates—6 g.; Cholesterol—36 mg.; Sodium—53 mg.

SALMON SPREAD

DAIRY

9 oz. fresh or canned boneless salmon
4 oz. smoked salmon
¼ small red onion
1½ tbsp. lemon juice

⅓ cup plain nonfat yogurt
½ cup celery, thinly sliced
4 small green olives, finely chopped

In a food processor or blender, process all of the salmon, red onion, lemon juice, and yogurt until smooth. Transfer to a bowl and mix in the celery and olives. Serves 4.

Serving suggestion: Spread thin on a half matzah or Matzah Snack Crackers. It doesn't take much to flavor the matzah because this spread is so flavor-packed.

Calories—137; Saturated fat—1 g.; Total fat—6 g.; Carbohydrates—3 g.; Cholesterol—42 mg.; Sodium—1032 mg.

Chicken, Turkey, and Beef

CHICKEN IN ORANGE SAUCE

The marriage of orange and chicken is a natural. The Israelis have known about this appealing combination for a long time. Now many of us have opted for this taste, instead of frying chicken in oil.

6 4-oz. chicken breast halves, skinned
3 tbsp. orange juice concentrate, thawed
1 cup defatted chicken broth or water
3 whole cloves

1 3-inch cinnamon stick
⅛ tsp. black pepper
Pinch cayenne pepper to taste
1½ tsp. potato starch
Orange slices for garnish
Parsley sprigs

In a nonstick skillet, over medium-high heat, brown the chicken breasts on both sides in the orange juice concentrate and ¼ cup of the broth for about 15-20 minutes.

Add the cloves, cinnamon stick, pepper, cayenne, and ½ cup of the broth. Bring to a boil. Reduce the heat to medium-low, cover, and simmer for 7-10 minutes or until the chicken is no longer pink inside.

With the remaining ¼ cup broth, blend in the potato starch and stir until smooth. Add this mixture to the skillet and stir until the gravy thickens and begins to bubble. Arrange the chicken on a platter and pour the sauce over all or pass the sauce around to individual plates. Garnish with the orange slices and parsley. Serves 4-6.

Calories—132; Saturated fat—0 g.; Total fat—2 g.; Carbohydrates—1 g.; Cholesterol—68 mg.; Sodium—89 mg.

CHICKEN, TURKEY, AND BEEF

CHICKEN WITH OLIVES

MEAT

My sister-in-law, Joelle Hankin, was born in Algeria, grew up in France, and now lives in South Carolina! Her family's Sephardic cooking is typical of the Algerian Jewish community but with a French influence. Joelle makes this Chicken with Olives every Pesach, and, being Sephardic, serves it with rice. It's a delicious dish and Ashkenazim may wish to serve it over sliced boiled new potatoes.

Cooking spray
6 4-oz. skinless boneless chicken breast halves
2 garlic cloves, halved
2 onions, thinly sliced
1 lb. whole mushrooms, cleaned
4 carrots, sliced diagonally

20 small green olives, sliced in half
2 lemons, quartered
½ cup dry white wine
¼ cup water
Black pepper to taste

Coat a large pot with the cooking spray. Rub the chicken with the garlic cloves.

Over medium heat, saute the chicken until browned on both sides with the onion slices. Add a little water if needed to prevent sticking.

Add the remaining ingredients, reduce heat, and simmer covered 1 hour, or until much of the liquid has evaporated. Serves 5-6.

Calories—233; Saturated fat—1 g.; Total fat—4 g.; Carbohydrates—17 g.; Cholesterol—68 mg.; Sodium—380 mg.

GINGERED PINEAPPLE CHICKEN WITH VEGETABLES

MEAT

The blend of the colorful vegetables and chicken makes a beautiful platter. This is versatile in that you may increase or decrease the amount of vegetables depending upon the size of your company.

1 tsp. ground ginger
½ cup cake meal
6 4-oz. boneless chicken breast
   halves, skinned
Cooking spray
3 medium sweet potatoes, peeled
3 large carrots

½ green pepper
½ cup pineapple chunks
1 cup celery, sliced
1 cup pineapple juice
1 cup chicken broth
½ tsp. garlic powder
½ tsp. ground ginger

Place your oven rack on the bottom slot. Preheat the oven to 475 degrees.

In a plastic bag, combine the ginger with the cake meal. Drop 2 pieces of chicken at a time into the bag and shake to coat. Spray a nonstick baking pan with the cooking spray. Arrange the coated chicken in a single layer and bake for approximately 10 minutes on each side to lightly brown it.

Meanwhile, slice the vegetables and transfer to a large baking dish. Remove the chicken from the oven and place with the vegetables in baking dish.

Combine the pineapple juice, chicken broth, garlic powder, and ginger and pour over the chicken and vegetables. Reduce the heat to 350 degrees and bake for 30 minutes or until the vegetables are tender and chicken is no longer pink. Serve on a large platter with the chicken in the middle surrounded by the vegetables. Serves 6.

Calories—303; Saturated fat—0 g.; Total fat—2 g.; Carbohydrates—40 g.; Cholesterol—68 mg.; Sodium—179 mg.

SPINACH CHICKEN ROLLS IN TOMATO SAUCE

Cooking spray
1 lb. fresh spinach, cleaned and
  chopped
1/3 cup mushrooms, chopped
1 clove garlic
1½ tsp. dry basil
4 to 6 4-oz. boneless chicken
  breast halves, skinned

4 to 6 1-oz. thin slices smoked
  white turkey
1 11-oz. can Italian-style tomato
  sauce or 1 recipe Italian
  Tomato Sauce

Coat a saute pan with the cooking spray and combine the spinach, mushrooms, garlic, and basil. Cover and cook over medium heat until the spinach wilts.

Preheat the oven to 350 degrees.

Flatten or pound out chicken between plastic wrap sheets to about ¼-inch thick. Lay a slice of smoked turkey to fit each chicken breast.

Divide the spinach mixture evenly onto each chicken breast. Fold over 2 short sides by 1 inch. Then roll the meat as you would a jelly roll and secure with tooth-picks. Place in a baking dish and bake uncovered for 20 minutes. Pour the sauce over the rolls and continue baking approximately 10 more minutes, or until the chicken is no longer pink and the sauce is bubbly. Serves 4.

Calories—169; Saturated fat—0 g.; Total fat—2 g.; Carbohydrates—7 g.; Cholesterol—69 mg.; Sodium—267 mg.

ITALIAN TOMATO SAUCE

1 cup chopped tomatoes
1 8-oz. can low sodium tomato
  sauce
3 tbsp. dry red wine

½ tsp. dry basil
½ tsp. dry oregano
⅛ tsp. black pepper

Combine all of the ingredients in a saucepan. Bring to a boil, reduce the heat, and simmer for 20 minutes. Makes 2½ cups.

PAPRIKA OVEN-FRIED CHICKEN

MEAT

**6 4-oz. skinless chicken breast
halves**
¼ cup cake meal
½ cup matzah meal
**2 tbsp. sesame seeds, toasted
(optional for Sephardim)**

¼ tsp. black pepper
2 tbsp. paprika
¼ tsp. salt
**½ cup orange juice mixed with 1
egg white**
Cooking spray

Preheat the oven to 400 degrees.

Place chicken in a bowl of cold water. Set aside.

In a plastic or paper bag, combine the cake meal, matzah meal, sesame seeds, black pepper, paprika, and salt.

Dip the chicken pieces in the orange juice-egg white mixture, then place a couple of pieces at a time into the bag and shake to coat the chicken.

Generously coat a baking sheet with cooking spray and place in the oven on the bottom rack. Arrange the chicken in a single layer. Bake for 20 minutes. Turn the chicken and bake for an additional 15-20 minutes, or until the chicken is no longer pink inside. Serves 4-6.

Calories—219; Saturated fat—1 g.; Total fat—3 g.; Carbohydrates—19 g.; Cholesterol—68 mg.; Sodium: 226 mg.

OVEN FRY CHICKEN

With Yam Crispies or Oven Fries, this is a real family-pleaser.

2½ lb. skinless chicken breasts
  and drumsticks
¼ cup cake meal
½ cup matzah meal
1 tbsp. potato starch
½ tsp. sugar
1 tsp. oregano

1 tsp. basil
½ tsp. paprika
½ tsp. onion powder
½ tsp. garlic powder
Cooking spray
1 tbsp. oil

Preheat the oven to 400 degrees.

Place the chicken pieces in a large pot filled cold water. In a sealed plastic bag, shake together the cake meal, matzah meal, potato starch, sugar, oregano, basil, paprika, onion powder, and garlic powder.

Coat a baking sheet with the cooking spray and oil.

Shake 2-3 pieces of chicken at a time in the bag until all of the pieces are coated.

Lay the chicken on the baking sheet and spray the chicken with 1 coating of the cooking spray. Bake for 20 minutes. Turn the chicken over. Bake for 20 minutes longer or until the chicken is no longer pink inside. Serves 4.

Calories—427; Saturated fat—2 g.; Total fat—10 g.; Carbohydrates—20 g.; Cholesterol—193 mg.; Sodium—210 mg.

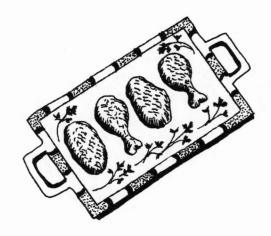

BARBECUE BROILED CHICKEN

MEAT

This features an easy sauce to go with a quick and easy dinner.

Cooking spray
½ onion, finely diced
1 garlic clove, minced
1½ cups tomato sauce
½ cup prune juice
3 tbsp. lemon juice

2 tbsp. brown sugar or sugar
¼ tsp. ground cloves
¼ tsp. powdered ginger
¼ tsp. black pepper
6-8 4 oz. boneless skinless chicken breast halves

Preheat the oven to broil.

Coat a nonstick skillet with the cooking spray. Over medium heat, lightly the brown onion and garlic. Add the remaining seasoning ingredients and simmer on low for about 5 minutes to meld the flavors.

Coat a broiler pan with the cooking spray. Brush the chicken with the sauce on each side as needed while broiling. Broil about 7 minutes on each side or until chicken is no longer pink. Serves 6-8.

Calories—169; Saturated fat—0 g.; Total fat—1 g.; Carbohydrates—11 g.; Cholesterol—68 mg.; Sodium—87 mg.

CHICKEN WITH BOK CHOY AND BROCCOLI

MEAT

1 broccoli stalk, trimmed, cut into florets
3 tbsp. dry white wine
½ lb. boneless chicken breast, cut into strips
1 tsp. oil
1½ tsp. finely minced ginger

1 small onion, cut into 8 wedges
8 oz. bok choy, leaves included, cut into 1-inch diagonal pieces
½ cup chicken broth
1½ tsp. potato starch
⅛ tsp. red pepper flakes
Dash black pepper

Parboil the broccoli florets for 1 minute. Drain and set aside.

Heat a large nonstick frying pan over medium-high heat. Add the wine, then the chicken, and stir-fry until the chicken loses its pink. Add a small amount of water if needed to prevent sticking. Remove from the pan. Set aside.

In same pan, heat the oil and stir-fry the ginger, broccoli, onion, and bok choy. Add a small amount of water and cover for about 2 minutes to steam the vegetables.

In a small bowl, blend the chicken broth, potato starch, red pepper flakes, and black pepper. Return the chicken to the pan. Reduce the heat to medium-low and stir the broth mixture into the chicken and vegetables until the sauce is heated through and thickens slightly. Serves 4.

Serving suggestion: Serve over Spaghetti Squash or mashed potatoes.

Calories—113; Saturated fat—0 g.; Total fat—2 g.; Carbohydrates—5 g.; Cholesterol—33 mg.; Sodium—131 mg.

QUICK CHICKEN POTATO TOPPER

MEAT

For a quick dinner after work with leftover chicken.

4 baking potatoes
2 cups mushrooms, sliced
½ cup green peppers, diced
⅓ cup scallions, chopped
½ cup low-calorie Passover Italian salad dressing

1 cup cooked chicken breast or leftover chicken, skinned and diced

Bake the potatoes until tender.

In a nonstick skillet over medium heat, saute the mushrooms, green peppers, and green onions with ¼ cup of the salad dressing until most of the dressing is absorbed. Add the chicken and the remainder of the salad dressing to the skillet and stir until heated through.

Split the baked potatoes open and mash a little. Spoon the chicken topping over the potatoes. Serves 4.

Calories—281; Saturated fat—0 g.; Total fat—1 g.; Carbohydrates—55 g.; Cholesterol—19 mg.; Sodium—458 mg.

CHICKEN CASSEROLE

What to do with the chicken from the matzah ball soup.

2 cups cooked white-meat chicken, cut into small cubes
4 egg whites
1 cup low-sodium tomato sauce
½ cup onions, chopped
2 tsp. chopped fresh basil, or 1½ tsp. dry basil
1 tbsp. parsley, chopped
1 garlic clove, chopped (optional)

1 tbsp. capers (optional)
⅛ tsp. black pepper, or to taste
2 red bell peppers, roasted (see the Roasted Peppers recipe), cut into strips, and sliced in half
3 matzahs
1 cup chicken broth
Cooking spray

Preheat the oven to 375 degrees.

In a bowl combine the chicken, egg whites, ½ cup of the tomato sauce, onion, basil, parsley, garlic, capers, black pepper, and roasted peppers.

In a shallow dish, dip the first matzah into the broth to moisten but do not soak. Spray an 8-by-8-inch baking dish with cooking spray. Place the matzah in the pan and spread ½ of the chicken mixture evenly over it.

Dip the next matzah into the broth and layer. Layer the remaining chicken mixture and cover with the last moistened matzah. Cover with foil and bake in the preheated oven for 20 minutes. Remove the foil and pour the remaining tomato sauce over the top and continue baking 15 minutes longer. Serves 4.

Calories—116; Saturated fat—0 g.; Total fat—2 g.; Carbohydrates—5 g.; Cholesterol—38 mg.; Sodium—179 mg.

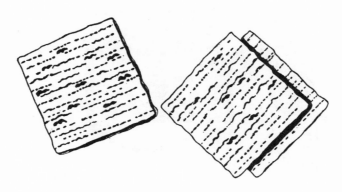

HEARTY CHICKEN CHOLENT

MEAT

A lowfat Pesadige version of the traditional Shabbat slow-cooking stew.

6 4-oz. boneless chicken breast
   halves, each cut in half
1 large onion, cut into wedges
2 tsp. paprika
1 tsp. salt
1 tsp. black pepper

2 tsp. garlic powder
3 tbsp. potato starch
4 baking potatoes, peeled, quartered
5 medium carrots, sliced

Preheat the oven to 250 degrees.
Place the chicken and onions in the center of a large pot or Dutch oven.
Combine the seasonings with the potato starch and sprinkle over the chicken.
Layer the baking potatoes and carrots over chicken.

MEATBALLS

1 lb. lean ground turkey meat or
   extra lean ground beef
2 tbsp. matzah meal
½ tsp. onion powder

½ tsp. garlic powder
1 tsp. black pepper
2 egg whites

Make meatballs and layer over potatoes and carrots.

4 medium sweet potatoes,
   peeled, quartered
2 garlic cloves, chopped

½ tsp. tumeric (optional)
4 cups boiling water

Top the chicken, vegetables, and meatballs with the sweet potatoes and garlic cloves and sprinkle with the tumeric. Pour boiling water over all of it. Cover and bake at 250 degrees before Shabbat until Shabbat lunch.

If necessary, add a small amount of water that has been kept hot for Shabbat. Serves 8.

Calories—424; Saturated fat—1 g.; Total fat—3 g.; Carbohydrates—60 g.; Cholesterol—85 mg.; Sodium—430 mg.

ROAST TURKEY BREAST

MEAT

1 5-6 lb. turkey breast
2 garlic cloves, chopped
Lemon pepper
Paprika
1 large onion, chopped
1 large carrot, shredded

1 large celery stalk and leaves, chopped
1 garlic clove, chopped
1 cup chicken broth or semidry white wine
3 peppercorns

Preheat the oven to 450 degrees.

Rub the entire surface of the turkey breast with the garlic cloves. Sprinkle with the lemon pepper and paprika. Place the onion, carrot, celery, and clove on the bottom of the roasting pan. Place the turkey on top. Roast uncovered at 450 degrees for 20 minutes.

Add the chicken broth or wine. Reduce the temperature to 350 degrees and cover the roasting pan. Continue cooking according to poundage and make sure there is always enough liquid to cover bottom of pan.

Cool before slicing. You may want to slice the turkey, then pour the juices over it to serve. I like the cooked vegetables from the pan. They add color and more flavor. You may choose to strain the liquid. Serves 10-12.

Made with chicken broth: Calories—233; Saturated fat—1 g.; Total fat—3 g.; Carbohydrates—5 g.; Cholesterol—113 mg.; Sodium—263 mg.

Made with semidry white wine: Calories—245; Saturated fat—1 g.; Total fat—3 g.; Carbohydrates—5 g.; Cholesterol—113 mg.; Sodium—258 mg.

SAUCY TURKEY MEATBALLS

MEATBALLS

Cooking spray
1 cup cabbage, shredded
3 green onions, finely chopped,
  including tops
1 clove garlic, minced

1 lb. lean ground white turkey
¼ cup matzah meal
1 egg white
¼ tsp. black pepper

Coat the bottom of a heavy saute pan with the cooking spray. Saute the cabbage, onions, and garlic for 2-3 minutes. Remove and combine in a bowl with the remaining ingredients. Wet hands to form meatballs and place in the same skillet and brown lightly on all sides for 8-10 minutes. Meanwhile, prepare the sauce.

SAUCE

Cooking spray
1 large onion, chopped
1 cup carrots, diced
2 cups tomato sauce

½ cup water
½ tsp. basil
2 tbsp. dry red wine

In a 4-quart pot, bottom-coated with cooking spray, saute the onion and carrots for about 3-4 minutes. Add the remaining sauce ingredients. Transfer the meatballs into the pot. Cover and simmer together for about 10 minutes to meld flavors. Serves 4.

Calories—216; Saturated fat—1 g.; Total fat—2 g.; Carbohydrates—16 g.; Cholesterol—68 mg.; Sodium—102 mg.

MEDITERRANEAN KABOBS

1½ lb. ground turkey or lean
  ground beef
½ lb. ground lamb
1 medium onion, chopped

2-3 tbsp. chopped cilantro
1 tsp. cumin
¼ cup cold water

Mix all of the ingredients together. Form into oval patties.

Broil or grill, turning side to side, for 8-10 minutes or until the meat is no longer pink. Serves 4.

Calories—273; Saturated fat—4 g.; Total fat—8 g.; Carbohydrates—0 g.; Cholesterol—143 mg.; Sodium—141 mg.

MEAT KNISHES

MEAT

A hearty, yet heart-healthy satisfying meal.

MEAT FILLING

Cooking spray
½ lb. lean ground chicken, turkey, or extra-lean ground beef
¼ cup onion, finely chopped

1 tbsp. freshly chopped parsley or 1 tsp. dried parsley
1 garlic clove, chopped
¼ tsp. black pepper

Coat a nonstick skillet with the cooking spray. Over medium heat, cook the filling ingredients until the meat is no longer pink. Set aside.

KNISH

1 heaping cup mashed potatoes
⅓ cup matzah meal or cake meal
2 tbsp. potato starch
½ small onion, finely chopped

2 egg whites or ¼ cup Passover egg substitute
½ tsp. black pepper
¼ tsp. salt

Preheat the oven to 375 degrees.

In a bowl, combine the knish ingredients and knead together. Divide the dough into 6 balls and flatten each. Divide the meat mixture evenly onto each circle; fold over and press edges to seal.

Generously coat a baking sheet with the cooking spray. Arrange the knishes in a single layer and place the baking sheet on the bottom rack of the oven. Bake at 375 degrees for about 15 minutes on each side. Serve hot. Serves 3 (2 knishes each).

Calories—127; Saturated fat—1 g.; Total fat—3 g.; Carbohydrates—9 g.; Cholesterol—26 mg.; Sodium—127 mg.

POTATO-CROWNED MEATLOAF

LOAF

1 lb. ground skinless turkey
  breast
1 egg white
3 tbsp. tomato paste
2 tsp. horseradish
½ tsp. paprika
⅛ tsp. black pepper

Cooking spray
¼ cup shallots or onions,
  chopped
1 cup chopped raw vegetables
  such as celery, bell pepper, or
  shredded carrots
⅔ cup matzah meal

Preheat the oven to 350 degrees.

In a large bowl, combine the first 6 ingredients. Set aside.

Coat a nonstick skillet with the cooking spray and saute the shallots and celery over medium heat for 2-3 minutes. Transfer to the ground turkey mixture and mix in the matzah meal thoroughly.

Form into a loaf on a baking sheet and bake for 30 minutes. Meanwhile, prepare the crown.

CROWN

3 medium potatoes, boiled
2 tsp. dry minced onions
¾ cup chicken broth

Cayenne pepper to taste
Paprika

In a medium bowl, mash the potatoes to equal 2 cups. Mix the potatoes with the onions, chicken broth, and cayenne pepper and mash.

"Ice" the meatloaf with the mashed potatoes. Turn the oven to broil and return the meatloaf to the oven to broil until the potatoes are golden brown. Sprinkle with the paprika and serve. Serves 6-8.

Variation: Use ½ lb. lean ground beef and ½ lb. lean ground turkey.

Calories—408; Saturated fat—1 g.; Total fat—3 g.; Carbohydrates—60 mg.; Cholesterol—68 mg.; Sodium—150 mg.

STUFFED BELL PEPPERS

4 large bell peppers, red, green, yellow, or combination
Cooking spray
1 medium onion, finely chopped
½ large red bell pepper, chopped
1 lb. lean ground turkey
1-2 large raw potatoes, shredded (equaling 1½ cups)
1 tsp. cumin
1 tsp. coriander

½ tsp. black pepper
¼ tsp. salt (optional)
¼ tsp. basil
2 egg whites (optional)
2 cups low-sodium tomato sauce
¼ tsp. basil
⅛ tsp. black pepper
1 tsp. cumin
½ tsp. thyme

Preheat the oven to 350 degrees.

Halve each pepper lengthwise; core and seed them.

In a steamer, steam the peppers above boiling water until tender-crisp (6-8 minutes). Then arrange in a baking dish. Set aside.

Coat a large nonstick skillet with cooking spray and saute the onion and chopped red bell pepper for about 3-4 minutes over medium-high heat. Add the ground turkey, potatoes, and seasonings. Cook for about 7 minutes or until the turkey loses its pink color. Add the egg whites and continue to simmer on low.

Combine the tomato sauce, basil, black pepper, cumin, and thyme in a small saucepan over medium heat. Simmer for 5 minutes. Transfer ⅓ cup of the seasoned tomato sauce into the meat mixture.

Spoon the meat mixture into each pepper half. Top the peppers with remaining sauce. Bake uncovered for 20 minutes to heat through. Serves 4.

Variation: You may substitute 1 teaspoon basil and 1 teaspoon oregano for the cumin and coriander in the turkey mixture, and 1 teaspoon basil for the cumin in the sauce.

Calories—321; Saturated fat—1 g.; Total fat—3 g.; Carbohydrates—41 g.; Cholesterol—68 mg.; Sodium—133 mg.

PACIFIC RIM CHICKEN SALAD

MEAT

DRESSING

⅓ cup orange juice
¼ cup cider vinegar
2 tbsp. honey

1 tsp. fresh ginger, peeled and
shredded

Combine the dressing ingredients. Mix well to blend in honey.

CHICKEN SALAD

1 lb. cooked skinless chicken
breast, cut into strips
4 cups Chinese cabbage, slivered
1 small carrot, shredded
1 stalk celery, thinly sliced
1 scallion, finely chopped

½ red pepper, thinly sliced
½ green pepper, thinly sliced
⅓ cup mushrooms, sliced
2 tsp. toasted sesame seeds for
topping

In a large bowl, combine the chicken salad ingredients. Pour the dressing over the salad. Chill. Sprinkle the sesame seeds on top just before serving. Serves 4.

Calories—240; Saturated fat—1 g.; Total fat—2 g.; Carbohydrates—25 g.; Cholesterol—66 mg.; Sodium—326 mg.

Vegetarian
Main Dishes

PESADIGE LASAGNA

DAIRY

This modern twist on an old standard is easier to make than it looks.
It is a beautiful dish and well worth the extra steps.

GREEN LAYER

10 oz. frozen spinach, thawed
   and drained, or 1 lb. fresh
   spinach, steamed and chopped
½ cup parsley, chopped

1 green onion, chopped
½ tsp. oregano
1 small zucchini, thinly sliced

In a small bowl, combine all of the ingredients except the zucchini, but have the zucchini nearby—it will be placed directly on top of this layer.

WHITE LAYER

1 cup lowfat Ricotta cheese
1 garlic clove, finely chopped

½ tsp. oregano

In a small bowl, combine all of the ingredients.

RED LAYER

2 roasted red peppers, sliced
   (see the Roasted Peppers
   recipe)
1 small onion, chopped
1 tsp. oil

1 garlic clove, finely chopped
1 tsp. basil
¼ tsp. black pepper
1 can (10½ oz.) low-sodium
   tomato sauce

While the peppers are under the broiler, saute the onions in oil until lightly brown. Then combine all of the remaining ingredients in a bowl.

MATZAH LAYER

3 matzahs
Cooking spray

White Sauce (recipe follows)

Preheat the oven to 350 degrees.

Dip the first matzah in cold water. Spray a 9-by-9-inch baking pan with the cooking spray. Lay the first matzah in the pan and spread the Green Layer to the edges of the matzah. Layer the zucchini evenly over the top. Wet the second matzah and layer it in the pan. Then spread the White Layer to the edges of the matzah. Wet the third matzah and layer it in the pan. Place the Red Layer to the edges of the matzah. Make the White Sauce.

WHITE SAUCE

1¼ cups skim milk
⅛ tsp. nutmeg
⅛ tsp. black pepper

1 tbsp. potato starch
2 tbsp. Parmesan cheese

In a small saucepan, over medium-high heat, heat 1 cup of the skim milk, nutmeg, and black pepper. In a small bowl, blend the potato starch and remaining milk into the saucepan and stir until the sauce thickens. Remove from heat and stir in the Parmesan cheese. Pour the White Sauce over the lasagna. Bake at 350 degrees 50-60 minutes. Serves 4.

Calories—260; Saturated fat—1 g.; Total fat—3 g.; Carbohydrates—40 g.; Cholesterol—11 mg.; Sodium—531 mg.

SPICY VEGGIE COMBO

*This is a spicy combination of vegetables that is similar
to a vegetarian version of fajitas that my brother Glenn enjoys.
The portobello mushrooms have a meaty texture.*

Cooking spray
1 tsp. oil
2 onions, thinly sliced
3 garlic cloves, chopped
1 roasted jalapeno pepper (see
   the Roasted Peppers recipe),
   chopped
1 green bell pepper, thinly sliced
1 yellow bell pepper, thinly sliced

1 red bell pepper, thinly sliced
½ lb. portobello mushrooms,
   sliced ¼-inch thick
¼ cup red wine
¼ cup cilantro, chopped
8 oz. yolk-free egg noodles (⅔ of
   a 12-oz. package), cooked
   according to package directions

Coat a large nonstick skillet with the cooking spray and add the oil. Heat the skillet over medium-high heat and saute the onions, garlic, and jalapeno for 2-3 minutes. Add the peppers, mushrooms, and wine. Saute until tender. Mix in the cilantro and serve over the noodles. Serves 4.

Variation: Omit the cilantro and combine Spicy Veggie Combo with Italian Tomato Sauce and serve over noodles.

Calories—301; Saturated fat—0 g.; Total fat—2 g.; Carbohydrates—48 g.; Cholesterol—0 mg.; Sodium—49 mg.

INDIAN STEW

PAREVE

This dish is inspired by my friendship with Carla Pai, originally from Bombay. She enjoys sharing her spicy cuisine and its exotic flavors with me. These spices are also common to Sephardic cooking. If you want it even spicier, add a finely chopped jalapeno pepper to the sauce. That's what Carla would do.

SAUCE

1 small butternut squash, peeled
  and cut into chunks
1 cup water or Vegetable Stock
1½ tsp. fresh ginger, peeled and
  minced

2 garlic cloves, minced
¾ tsp. cumin
½ tsp. tumeric
⅛-¼ tsp. crushed red pepper, or
  to taste

Steam or boil the squash until tender.

In a bowl, mash squash (should equal about 1 cup when mashed) with the water and add the remaining ingredients. Mix into the stew mixture.

STEW

2 tsp. oil
1 onion, thinly sliced
1 eggplant, peeled and cubed
2 medium carrots, sliced

½ small cauliflower, cut into florets
2 small zucchini
Black pepper to taste
Cilantro leaves for garnish

Over medium-high heat, add the oil to a large nonstick saute pan and lightly brown the onions. Add the eggplant and saute for another 5 minutes. Add the carrots and cauliflower. Add a small amount of water if needed to prevent sticking. Cover and reduce heat. Simmer for 15 minutes. Add the zucchini and continue to

simmer for another 10 minutes or until the vegetables are tender. Sprinkle with black pepper. Garnish with cilantro leaves. Serves 4.

Variation: Add more water or vegetable stock to the sauce if a thinner sauce is desired.

Calories—265; Saturated fat—0 g.; Total fat—3 g.; Carbohydrates—53 g.; Cholesterol—0 mg.; Sodium—36 mg.

VEGETABLE PIZZA

DAIRY

PIZZA CRUST

4 small potatoes, peeled, boiled, and mashed, equaling 2 cups
1 cup cake meal
¼ tsp. salt
2 egg whites
Cooking spray

Preheat the oven to 375 degrees.
Combine the first 4 ingredients and knead until well blended. Coat an aluminum pizza pan or a baking sheet with the cooking spray. Spread the potato mixture to the sides of the pan. Bake at 375 degrees for about 15 minutes.

VEGETABLE TOPPING

1 cup low-sodium tomato sauce
1 small tomato, thinly sliced
1 roasted red pepper (see the Roasted Peppers recipe), thinly sliced
4 oz. mushrooms, sliced
1½ tsp. dry basil
¼ cup lowfat mozzarella cheese
1 tbsp. Parmesan cheese

Spread the tomato sauce evenly over the crust. Arrange the tomato slices, red peppers, and mushrooms on top. Sprinkle with basil and mozzarella cheese and top with the Parmesan cheese. Place under the broiler until the cheese melts. Serves 4-6.

Variation: Other easy topping ideas include thinly sliced green pepper, zucchini, or onion; 4 black olives, diced chili peppers, and crushed red pepper flakes.

Calories—196; Saturated fat—1 g.; Total fat—1 g.; Carbohydrates—38 g.; Cholesterol—3 mg.; Sodium—161 mg.

SPINACH LEEK PIE

*If you want it more vitamin dense, make the crust with
1½ pounds of sweet potato.*

CRUST

Cooking spray
¾ lb. sweet potatoes, cooked
  and peeled

¾ lb. potatoes
½ cup nonfat plain yogurt

Preheat the oven to 375 degrees.

Coat a 9-by-11-inch baking dish with the cooking spray. Mash the potatoes together with the yogurt, and pat into the dish while spreading evenly over the bottom and up the sides of the dish to form a crust.

FILLING

Cooking spray
2 leeks, white part only, rinsed
  well and sliced
½ lb. mushrooms, sliced
2 garlic cloves, minced
¼ tsp. nutmeg

2 lb. spinach or 2 pkg. (10 oz.
  each) frozen chopped spinach,
  thawed and drained
½ cup of any kind of lowfat
  white cheese

In a large nonstick skillet coated with cooking spray, saute the leeks, mushrooms, and garlic over medium-high heat until the leeks soften. Spoon into the crust.

In same skillet, add the spinach. Reduce heat. Cover and steam until the spinach wilts. Add the nutmeg and chop the spinach. Spoon this evenly over the mushrooms and leeks. Sprinkle with the cheese.

Prepare egg mixture.

EGG MIXTURE

4 egg whites
1½ cups skim milk
¼ tsp. salt

⅛ tsp. black pepper
Paprika for garnish

In a bowl, mix the egg whites, milk, salt, and pepper. Pour over the pie. Top with a little paprika for color. Bake in the preheated oven for 35-40 minutes, until the top is firm to the touch. Serves 6.

Calories—276; Saturated fat—1 g.; Total fat—3 g.; Carbohydrates—46 g.; Cholesterol—7 mg.; Sodium—372 mg.

CAULIFLOWER LATKES

DAIRY

1 medium head cauliflower
2 egg whites
1 stalk celery, finely chopped
2 scallions, finely chopped
½ tsp. white horseradish
¼ tsp. paprika

⅛ tsp. black pepper
¼ cup cake meal
¼ cup lowfat white cheese
Cooking spray
1-1½ tsp. oil

Steam the cauliflower until tender. Mash; add the egg whites, celery, scallions, seasonings, cake meal, and cheese; and form into patties.

Coat a nonstick griddle with the cooking spray. Heat the griddle over medium heat then add ½ teaspoon of oil.

Brown the patties lightly on both sides. With each batch of latkes, coat the griddle with cooking spray and add ½ teaspoon of oil. Serves 4.

Calories—99; Saturated fat—1 g.; Total fat—3 g.; Carbohydrates—12 g.; Cholesterol—5 mg.; Sodium—270 mg.

BROCCOLI FRITTADA

¾ cup matzah farfel
Olive oil cooking spray
1 cup broccoli florets
½ onion, chopped
½ cup mushrooms, sliced
½ red pepper, chopped

6 jumbo egg whites
1 whole egg
½ tsp. basil or oregano
¼ cup of any kind of lowfat
   white cheese, shredded

Soften the farfel by soaking it in a bowl of cold water.

Coat a nonstick skillet with the cooking spray. Over medium heat, saute the broccoli and onions for about 3-4 minutes. If needed, spray another coating of cooking spray, add the mushrooms and red peppers, and saute for another minute.

In a bowl mix the egg whites, egg, and basil. Drain the farfel well, squeezing the extra water out, and add to the skillet.

Pour the egg mixture over the top of the vegetables. Reduce the heat to medium-low, cover, and cook for 15 minutes or until the eggs are almost set. Sprinkle with the cheese. Cover and continue to cook until the eggs are completely set and the cheese melts. Serves 4.

Calories—121; Saturated fat—1 g.; Total fat—3 g.; Carbohydrates—12 g.; Cholesterol—58 mg.; Sodium—157 mg.

ASPARAGUS AND POTATO BAKED FRITTADA

VEGETABLE MIXTURE

1 tsp. oil
2 cups unpeeled potatoes, diced
1 clove garlic, minced
½ cup water
2 cups fresh asparagus, sliced

into bite-sized pieces
½ cup green onions (including tops), chopped
1 tbsp. fresh dill, chopped

Preheat the oven to 400 degrees.

In a large nonstick skillet, over medium-high heat, saute the potatoes and garlic in the oil for about 5 minutes. Reduce heat to low, add the water, cover, and steam for 15 minutes, turning the potatoes once or twice.

Add the asparagus, green onions, and dill; continue to steam, covered, until the asparagus is tender-crisp, about 3-4 minutes.

EGG MIXTURE

6 jumbo egg whites
1 whole egg
1 cup lowfat cottage cheese
3 tbsp. Parmesan cheese, grated
3 tbsp. part skim mozzarella cheese, grated

¼ tsp. black pepper
¼ tsp. paprika
1 matzah, crumbled, water-soaked, squeezed dry
¼ cup lowfat cheese, grated (optional for topping)

In a bowl, mix the Egg Mixture ingredients (except the lowfat cheese for the topping). Add the Vegetable Mixture from the skillet and mix thoroughly.

Spray the bottoms and sides of a 9-by-13-inch baking pan with cooking spray. Pour the mixture evenly into the baking pan. Bake the frittada at 400 degrees until the eggs are almost set (about 15 minutes). Add the cheese and continue to bake for another 10 minutes or until the eggs are firm and the cheese is melted. Serves 6.

Calories—186; Saturated fat—2 g.; Total fat—4 g.; Carbohydrates—22 g.; Cholesterol—46 mg.; Sodium—136 mg.

RATATOUILLE

PAREVE

This is Ratatouille without the oil. The salad dressing not only helps to saute the vegetables but adds extra flavor.

Cooking spray
1 onion, chopped
3 garlic cloves, minced
½ cup low-calorie Passover
  Italian salad dressing
2 eggplants, peeled and cubed
2 zucchini, cubed
½ cup mushrooms, sliced

2 tomatoes. seeded and cubed
3 oz. capers, drained and rinsed
1 tsp. basil
Black pepper to taste
1 8-oz. can low-sodium tomato
  sauce
1 tsp. oregano or basil
1 tbsp. lemon juice

Coat a large, deep skillet or pot with the cooking spray. Over medium heat, saute the onion and garlic until the onion softens. Add the dressing and eggplant. Cook until soft. Add the zucchini and mushrooms; cook and stir occasionally for 15 minutes or until the vegetables are tender. Add the tomatoes, capers, basil, and black pepper.

Combine the tomato sauce, oregano, and lemon juice and mix into the vegetables. Ratatouille can be served warm or cold. Serves 4.

Calories—154; Saturated fat—1 g.; Total fat—6 g.; Carbohydrates—22 g.; Cholesterol—0 mg.; Sodium—376 mg.

EGGPLANT SAUCE OVER SPAGHETTI SQUASH

PAREVE

1 large spaghetti squash
1 medium onion, chopped
⅓ cup low-calorie Passover
  Italian salad dressing or dry
  red wine
1 large eggplant, peeled and
  cubed
½ cup mushrooms, sliced
¼ cup fresh parsley, chopped

1-2 garlic cloves, crushed
1 tsp. basil
1 tsp. oregano
⅛ tsp. black pepper
4 cups canned low-sodium tomatoes, chopped and undrained
¼ cup water
¼ cup dry red wine

If not prepared already, prepare the spaghetti squash according to the Spaghetti Squash recipe.

Meanwhile, in a nonstick skillet over medium-high heat, saute the onion in the Italian dressing for about 5 minutes.

Add the eggplant, mushrooms, parsley, and seasonings. Saute for 15 minutes or until the eggplant and mushrooms are soft. (A small amount of water may be added just to prevent sticking.)

Stir in the tomatoes, water, and wine. Reduce the heat to medium-low, cover, and simmer for 20 minutes.

To serve, use a fork to scoop out the spaghetti squash onto a serving platter or individual plates and spoon the eggplant sauce on top. Serves 4.

Calories—295; Saturated fat—1 g.; Total fat—5 g.; Carbohydrates—57 g.; Cholesterol—1 mg.; Sodium—247 mg.

SPAGHETTI SQUASH

**1 large spaghetti squash, halved
lengthwise**

Preheat the oven to 350 degrees. Place the squash cut side down in a baking dish. Bake in the preheated oven for about 1 hour or until tender. Remove the seeds and pull out the squash strands with a fork. Seves 4.

Serving suggestion: Use in Eggplant Sauce over Spaghetti Squash recipe.

Calories—40; Saturated fat—0 g.; Total fat—1 g.; Carbohydrates—6 g.; Cholesterol—0 mg.; Sodium—19 mg.

VEGETARIAN PRAKAS

**1 large head green cabbage
Cooking spray
1 onion, grated
1 carrot, grated
1 tsp. paprika
1/8 tsp. black pepper
4 matzahs, crumbled
1 medium potato, grated (about
   1 cup)
1/2 cup pineapple juice**

**3/4 cup crushed pineapple,
   undrained
1/2 cup raisins
2 egg whites
2 tbsp. ground almonds
16 oz. low-sodium tomato sauce
2 tbsp. lemon juice
Pinch sour salt (optional)
2 tbsp. honey**

Core the cabbage and parboil it in a large pot of water with the core side down for 15-20 minutes or until the leaves have softened slightly and can be easily removed.
   Preheat the oven to 350 degrees.
   Coat a large nonstick skillet with the cooking spray. Saute the onion, carrot, paprika, and black pepper over medium-high heat until the onion softens. Remove from heat and add the matzahs, potato, pineapple juice, pineapple, raisins, egg whites, and almonds. Mix until well moistened.
   Stuff the leaves with 2-3 tablespoons of the filling at the core end, folding core end

over once. Fold both sides in, and roll over again. Repeat procedure until filling is used up.

Shred remaining cabbage and spread half of it (reserving other half) on the bottom of a 9-by-13-inch casserole dish. Lay cabbage rolls, seam-side down, over the shredded cabbage. Top the rolls with the remaining shredded cabbage.

In a bowl, mix the tomato sauce, lemon juice, sour salt, and 1½ tablespoons of the honey. Pour this sauce over the cabbage rolls and cover with the foil. Bake in the preheated oven for about 1½ hours. During the last 10-15 minutes, drizzle the remaining honey for a glaze and continue baking uncovered. Serves 6.

Calories—346; Saturated fat—0 g.; Total fat—4 g.; Carbohydrates—69 g.; Cholesterol—0 mg.; Sodium—70 mg.

ARTICHOKES WITH MATZAH STUFFING

PAREVE

The Matzah Stuffing is delicious in itself—spoon into a greased baking dish and bake at 375 degrees for 30 minutes.

7 matzahs, finely broken into pieces
1¼ cups Vegetable Stock or water
½ lb. mushrooms, chopped
3 stalks celery, thinly sliced
¼ cup slivered almonds, toasted

1 medium tomato, chopped
¼ cup dry white wine
½ tsp. garlic powder
½ tsp. black pepper
6 Steamed Artichokes
1 recipe Artichoke Tomato Sauce (see below)

Preheat the oven to 375 degrees.

In a large bowl, combine matzah pieces with 1 cup of the stock or water. Set aside.

In a skillet, saute the mushrooms and celery in the remaining ¼ cup stock for about 7-8 minutes. Add to the matzahs along with the almonds, chopped tomato, wine, and seasonings.

When the artichokes are cool enough to handle, gently pull out the middle leaves of each artichoke. Scrape out the thistles with a spoon. Divide the stuffing mixture, stuff each artichoke, and top each with 1-2 tablespoons of Artichoke Tomato Sauce or to taste. Place the artichokes into a casserole dish and add a little water to the dish to cover the bottom. Bake uncovered about 30 minutes—but no longer or arti-chokes may dry out. Serves 6.

ARTICHOKE TOMATO SAUCE

8 oz. canned low-sodium tomato sauce
1 garlic clove, minced

¼ cup dry red wine
Pinch cayenne pepper

In a saucepan combine the ingredients and heat to warm them.

Calories—376; Saturated fat—1 g.; Total fat—5 g.; Carbohydrates—268 g.; Cholesterol—0 mg.; Sodium—914 mg.

Vegetables

MUSHROOMS SAUTEED IN WINE

PAREVE

This is elegant enough for company, simple enough for a family dinner.

Cooking spray
1 medium onion, sliced
2 garlic cloves, chopped
1¾ lb. mushrooms, sliced

¼ cup white wine
2 tbsp. lemon juice
2 tbsp. chopped fresh basil, or 2 tsp. dried basil

Coat a nonstick skillet with the cooking spray. Saute the onions and garlic over medium-high heat. Add the mushrooms and saute for about 10 minutes. Turn the heat down to medium and add the wine, lemon juice, and basil. Continue to saute and stir the mushrooms to pick up the flavors for another 5 minutes. Serves 4-5.

Calories—78; Saturated fat—0 g.; Total fat—1 g.; Carbohydrates—12 g.; Cholesterol—0 mg.; Sodium—8 mg.

ROASTED PEPPERS

PAREVE

*This is an all-purpose procedure for roasting peppers
such as red bell peppers, Anaheim chili peppers, and jalapeno peppers.*

Heat the oven to broil. Split the peppers in half. Cut off the tops and remove the seeds. Place the peppers under the broiler. Sear until the skin is blackened.

Remove and place in a brown paper bag and close to steam the vegetable. Let it sit for about 10-15 minutes, then remove the skin.

THREE-VEGETABLE MEDLEY

DAIRY

Cooking spray
½ cup onions, sliced
2 garlic cloves, minced
1½ cups broccoli florets
1½ cups carrots, cut into sticks

**1½ cups turnips, peeled and cut
  into sticks**
½ cup water
1½ tbsp. lemon juice
1 tbsp. Parmesan cheese

Coat a nonstick skillet with the cooking spray and saute the onions and garlic over medium-high heat. Add the broccoli, turnips, carrots, and water. Cover and simmer for about 8 minutes. Most of the water will evaporate. Add the lemon juice and Parmesan cheese. Serve warm. Serves 4-6.

Calories—37; Saturated fat—0 g.; Total fat—0 g.; Carbohydrates—7 g.; Cholesterol—1 mg.; Sodium—50 mg.

BROCCOFLOWER IN CHEESE SAUCE

DAIRY

If this hybrid vegetable is available in your area, try it! You may substitute cauliflower but the green of the broccoflower adds color to your table.

**1 head broccoflower, cut into
  florets**

**4 small new red potatoes, peeled
  and halved**

Steam the broccoflower florets until tender. Boil the potatoes until tender. Arrange the florets and potatoes on a serving platter. Prepare the cheese sauce.

CHEESE SAUCE

1½ cups skim milk
4 tsp. potato starch
⅛ tsp. black pepper
Pinch nutmeg

2 tbsp. Parmesan cheese
Paprika for garnish
**2 tbsp. fresh parsley, snipped,
  for garnish**

In a small saucepan, heat 1¼ cups of the milk. Combine the remaining ¼ cup of milk with the potato starch and pepper. Gradually add this mixture and whisk until the sauce thickens. Immediately remove from heat. Add the Parmesan cheese and stir until blended. Pour the cheese sauce over the vegetables. Sprinkle the top with paprika and garnish with parsley. Serves 4.

Calories—125; Saturated fat—1 g.; Total fat—1 g.; Carbohydrates—22 g.; Cholesterol—3 mg.; Sodium—102 mg.

ASPARAGUS WITH FLAIR

PAREVE

This is a beautiful presentation for any seder and the simplest to prepare.

2 lb. fresh asparagus
¼ cup water
½ cup celery, sliced
½ cup green onions, sliced

1 cup jicama, peeled and sliced
   into matchsticks
¾ cup red bell pepper, sliced
Juice of half a lemon

Snap off the tough ends of the asparagus.

Steam the asparagus for 7-8 minutes or until tender-crisp. Drain and set aside.

In a nonstick skillet, over medium-high heat, add the remaining ingredients. Cook the vegetables for about 5 minutes or until they are tender-crisp.

Arrange the asparagus on a platter. Spoon the vegetables over the hot asparagus and serve. Serves 6-8.

Calories—47; Saturated fat—0 g.; Total fat—0 g.; Carbohydrates—7 g.; Cholesterol—0 mg.; Sodium—17 mg.

CREAMED SPINACH

DAIRY

2 lb. spinach, cleaned and steamed
Cooking spray

4 scallions, finely chopped
2 garlic cloves, minced
White Sauce (see below)

While spinach is steaming, heat a large saute pan coated with the cooking spray. Over medium-high heat, saute the scallions and garlic until the garlic lightly browns.

Drain the spinach well and chop. Add to the scallions and garlic. Make the White Sauce.

WHITE SAUCE

¾ cup skim milk
½ tsp. coriander (optional)
Dash cayenne pepper (optional)

Dash black pepper
1 tbsp. Parmesan cheese
½ tbsp. potato starch

In a small saucepan, heat ½ cup of the milk, seasonings, and Parmesan cheese. Mix the remaining ¼ cup milk and potato starch together and stir into the milk. The sauce will thicken very quickly. Stir into the spinach mixture and serve. Serves 6.

Calories—66; Saturated fat—0 g.; Total fat—1 g.; Carbohydrates—9 g.; Cholesterol—1 mg.; Sodium—151 mg.

SIMPLE POTATO SPINACH CASSEROLE

DAIRY

This is a fast and easy throw-together side dish or main dish for the family.

4 baking potatoes, peeled and cubed
1 lb. fresh spinach
½ cup skim milk

¼ tsp. garlic powder
Black pepper to taste
¾ cup low-fat cottage cheese
3 tbsp. Parmesan cheese, grated

Steam the potatoes until tender.

While waiting for the potatoes, steam the fresh spinach several minutes until it wilts. Drain and chop.

In a bowl, mash the potatoes with the milk, garlic powder, and black pepper. Add the spinach to potatoes and mix. Place this mixture in an 8-by-8-inch broiler-proof casserole dish. Spread the cottage cheese over the top and sprinkle Parmesan cheese over all. Place casserole under the broiler until the cottage cheese melts and the Parmesan cheese browns. Serves 4.

Calories—315; Saturated fat—1 g.; Total fat—2 g.; Carbohydrates—58 g.; Cholesterol—5 mg.; Sodium—364 mg.

KISHKE

PAREVE

Cooking spray
1½ tbsp. oil
1 large onion, finely chopped
2 stalks celery
1 carrot
2 tsp. paprika
¾ tsp. salt

½ tsp. powdered ginger
½ tsp. garlic powder
¼ tsp. onion powder
½ tsp. black pepper
⅔ cup water
1½ cups cake meal
¼ cup matzah meal

Preheat the oven to 375 degrees.

Coat a nonstick skillet with the cooking spray. Over medium-high heat, saute the onion in the oil until lightly browned.

In a large bowl, grate the celery and carrot. Add the remaining ingredients. With wet hands, knead the mixture until it is well blended. Divide into 2 rolls, each approximately 2½ inches wide in diameter. Wrap a piece of foil around each roll and seal the tops and sides.

Place in the oven and bake for 40-45 minutes. If you want it browned, open foil halfway through baking. Serves 6-8.

Calories—105; Saturated fat—0 g.; Total fat—3 g.; Carbohydrates—16 g.; Cholesterol—0 mg.; Sodium—422 mg.

BROCCOLI KNISHES

PAREVE

These could be served as a side dish,
but are filling enough to be the main dish.

1 cup mashed potatoes
⅓ cup matzah meal
2 tbsp. potato starch
½ small onion, finely chopped
2 egg whites or ¼ cup Passover
egg substitute

½ tsp. black pepper
¼ tsp. salt
1 cup fresh or frozen broccoli,
steamed and finely chopped
Cooking spray

Preheat the oven to 375 degrees.

In a bowl combine the potatoes, matzah meal, potato starch, onion, egg whites, pepper, and salt and knead together. Divide the dough into 6 balls and flatten each. Divide the broccoli evenly onto each circle, fold over, and press edges to seal.

Generously coat a baking sheet with the cooking spray. Arrange the knishes in a single layer and place the baking sheet on the bottom rack of the oven. Bake for 15 minutes on each side. Serve hot. Serves 6.

Calories—82; Saturated fat—0 g.; Total fat—0 g.; Carbohydrates—15 g.; Cholesterol—0 mg.; Sodium—124 mg.

STIR-FRY CAULIFLOWER AND COMPANY

MEAT/PAREVE

1 medium head cauliflower, cut
  into florets
Cooking spray
2 cups mixed vegetables, any
  combination: red pepper,
  green pepper, green cabbage,
  red cabbage, and sliced zucchini, cut for stir-fry

2 scallions, sliced
½ cup mushrooms, sliced
½ cup Chicken or Vegetable
  Stock
½ tsp. potato starch
½ tsp. powdered ginger
⅛ tsp. black pepper

Parboil the cauliflower florets for 2-3 minutes. Drain.

Coat a nonstick skillet with the cooking spray. Saute the cauliflower and veggies for 5 minutes or until tender-crisp, adding a little water if necessary to prevent sticking.

In a bowl, mix the chicken broth, potato starch, ginger, and pepper. Stir into the vegetables and serve. Serves 4.

Calories—39; Saturated fat—0 g.; Total fat—0 g.; Carbohydrates—12 g.; Cholesterol—0 mg.; Sodium—18 mg.

STIR-FRY CHINESE CABBAGE

PAREVE

Cooking spray
½ tsp. oil
1½ tsp. fresh ginger, peeled and
  shredded
1 clove garlic, chopped

1 lb. napa (Chinese) cabbage, slivered
½ cup carrots, shredded
2 scallions, sliced
1½ tsp. vinegar

Coat a nonstick skillet with the cooking spray and add the oil. Over medium heat, saute the ginger and garlic for 1 minute. Add the remaining ingredients and continue stirring and sauteing for another 3-4 minutes until the cabbage wilts and is tender. Serves 4.

Calories—32; Saturated fat—0 g.; Total fat—1 g.; Carbohydrates—4 g.; Cholesterol—0 mg.; Sodium—79 mg.

EGG ROLLS

PAREVE/MEAT

*This goes with a complete Chinese meal—meat or vegetarian.
Start with Chinese Hot and Sour Soup. Follow with Chicken
with Bok Choy and Broccoli and a vegetable side dish of Cauliflower
Stir-Fry and Company or Stir-Fry Chinese Cabbage.*

EGG ROLL SKIN

½ cup Passover egg substitute   ½ cup cake meal
¾ cup water   Cooking spray

In a medium bowl, beat the egg substitute, water, and cake meal until smooth.
Coat a 7-inch nonstick saute pan with the cooking spray and heat it over medium heat until it is hot. Pour a scant ¼ cup (about 3 tablespoons) of batter at a time into the pan, tipping the pan until the batter spreads. Cook until the top appears dry. Turn egg roll skin cooked side up onto a platter or waxed paper. Repeat the procedure until the batter is used up. It will yield 1 dozen blintzes. Prepare filling.

FILLING

2 cups cabbage, shredded   3 scallions, chopped
½ cup carrots, shredded   1 cup cooked skinless chicken
½ cup bamboo shoots   breast, slivered (optional)
½ cup celery, finely sliced   Black pepper to taste

Combine the filling ingredients.

Cooking spray   2 tbsp. oil

Coat a large nonstick saute pan with the cooking spray. Over medium high, saute the vegetables until wilted.
Spoon about 1 tablespoon of the filling on the end of egg roll skin nearest you. Roll over once, fold the sides in toward the middle, and complete the roll. To brown the egg rolls, coat the same pan with more cooking spray. Over medium heat, add 1 tablespoon of oil and brown 6 rolls at a time on each side, seam side down. If a little oil is needed for the flip side, add about 1 teaspoon of more oil. Serve with kosher-for-Passover duck sauce. Makes 1 dozen.

Per egg roll: Calories—33; Saturated fat—0 g.; Total fat—2 g.; Carbohydrates—2 g.; Cholesterol—0 mg.; Sodium—24 mg.

RED ONIONS AND CABBAGE

PAREVE

An old standby recipe that's always tasty.

1 tsp. oil
1 cup sweet red onion, sliced
½ medium head (3-4 cups) red cabbage, slivered
½ cup apple juice

2 tart green apples, unpeeled and thinly sliced
1 tbsp. apple cider vinegar or lemon juice
1 tsp. caraway seeds (optional)

Heat the oil in a large nonstick skillet over medium heat and saute the onions until softened. Add the cabbage and apple juice; cover and simmer for 10 minutes. Add the apples, vinegar, and caraway seeds. Continue to simmer in a covered skillet for another 15 minutes. Add water if needed to prevent sticking. Serve warm. Serves 4.

Calories—116; Saturated fat—0 g.; Total fat—2 g.; Carbohydrates—23 g.; Cholesterol—0 mg.; Sodium—15 mg.

ZUCCHINI-CARROT STUFFED ACORN SQUASH

PAREVE

2 acorn squash, halved, seeded
Water
4 carrots, sliced

2 medium zucchini, sliced
½ cup crushed pineapple
¼ tsp. nutmeg

Preheat the oven to 350 degrees.

Place the squash cut-side down in a shallow baking pan filled with water to cover the bottom. Bake in the preheated oven for about 40 minutes or until tender.

Meanwhile steam the carrots and zucchini for 10 minutes or until tender. Stir in the pineapple and nutmeg.

Turn the squash halves upright. Spoon the mixture evenly into the squash halves. Return to the oven to heat through. Serves 4.

Calories—166; Saturated fat—0 g.; Total fat—1 g.; Carbohydrates—37 g.; Cholesterol—0 mg.; Sodium—34 mg.

ZUCCHINI TOMATO DUET

Sometimes the simplest recipe is the most elegant.

2 medium zucchini, cut into ½-inch slices
3 tbsp. water
2 tomatoes, cut into wedges
1½ tsp. oil
2 tbsp. lemon juice
⅛ tsp. salt

1 tbsp. fresh basil chopped or 1 tsp. dry basil
¼ tsp. black pepper, or to taste
½ tsp. lemon rind, grated
1 tbsp. Parmesan cheese, grated (optional)

In a saucepan, steam the zucchini in the water until tender-crisp. Remove from heat and add the tomatoes. Combine the oil and lemon juice. Drizzle over the vegetables and toss lightly. Add the basil, salt, pepper, and lemon rind.

Return to medium-low heat. Cover and simmer for 2-3 minutes or until the zucchini is tender and the flavors meld. Serve with the Parmesan cheese sprinkled on the top. Serves 4.

Calories—50; Saturated fat—0 g.; Total fat—3 g.; Carbohydrates—5 g.; Cholesterol—0 mg.; Sodium—80 mg.

JOELLE'S ALGERIAN CARROTS

PAREVE

This is one of Joelle's specialties. She uses 1 tablespoon of harissa—
a paste of dried red chili peppers seasoned with cumin, coriander, and garlic—
which is available in Middle Eastern markets. I found that roasting a jalapeno
pepper captures the zing this recipe calls for.

1 jalapeno pepper, roasted (see the Roasted Peppers recipe)	1½ tbsp. cumin
	1½ tbsp. paprika
1 lb. carrots, diagonally sliced	1½ tbsp. water
6 garlic cloves, crushed	½ cup white vinegar
½ tbsp. oil	½ cup water

After roasting the pepper, finely chop it.

In a saucepan, steam the carrots just until tender-crisp. Set aside.

In a large nonstick saute pan, saute the garlic in the oil for 1 minute. Mix in the jalapeno pepper, cumin, paprika, and water to make a paste. Add the vinegar, additional water, and carrots to the saute pan and stir until the mixture is well blended. Continue to cook and stir until most of the water has evaporated. Transfer into a bowl and chill before serving. Serves 8.

Calories—54; Saturated fat—0 g,; Total fat—1 g.; Carbohydrates—9 g.; Cholesterol—0 mg.; Sodium—23 mg.

SIMPLE PINEAPPLE CARROTS

PAREVE

3 cups carrots, cut into match-sticks
¾ cup pineapple juice
1 tsp. potato starch

½ tsp. ginger
½ cup pineapple small chunks or tidbits

In a saucepan, combine the carrots and ½ cup of the pineapple juice and bring to a boil. Reduce the heat, cover, and simmer until tender.

Meanwhile, in a small bowl, mix together the potato starch, remaining pineapple juice, and ginger. Stir into the carrot mixture along with the pineapple chunks and heat through until the juices thicken. Serves 4.

Calories—109; Saturated fat—0 g.; Total fat—0 g.; Carbohydrates—25 g.; Cholesterol—0 mg.; Sodium—30 mg.

POTATO PUFFS

This is a popular side dish with my company.

4 medium potatoes, peeled and
cooked
2 medium carrots, grated
½ cup scallions, finely chopped
3 tbsp. fresh parsley, finely
snipped

¾ cup chicken broth
¼ tsp. salt (or salt substitute)
¼ tsp. white pepper
2 egg whites
1 tsp. oil

Preheat the oven to 350 degrees.

In a bowl, mash the potatoes and set aside.

Place the carrots in a saucepan. Cover and steam for 5 minutes. Add the scallions and continue to steam for 1 minute. Add to the potatoes.

Mix the chicken broth, parsley, salt, and white pepper into the potatoes.

In a separate bowl, beat the egg whites until stiff but not dry. Fold into the potato mixture.

Spread the oil evenly over a nonstick baking sheet and spoon heaping tablespoonfuls of the potato mixture onto the sheet. Bake in the preheated oven for 30 minutes until lightly brown. Serves 4-6.

Variation: To serve as mashed potatoes, omit the egg whites and add 1-2 roasted garlic cloves. For a dairy meal, substitute a little skim milk for the chicken broth. Add enough milk to moisten the potatoes to the desired consistency.

Calories—266; Saturated fat—0 g.; Total fat—2 g.; Carbohydrates—54 g.; Cholesterol—0 mg.; Sodium—277 mg.

SKILLET HOME FRIES

3½ cups potatoes, unpeeled, diced
Water
Cooking spray
2 tsp. oil

1 tbsp. paprika
¾ tsp. salt or salt substitute
¼ tsp. pepper
1 tbsp. matzah meal

Place the diced potatoes in a saucepan. Cover with water and boil for 15 minutes or until the potatoes are tender-crisp. Drain. Transfer to a bowl and set aside.

Coat a nonstick skillet with the cooking spray. Heat the skillet to medium and add the oil.

Toss the paprika, salt, pepper, and matzah meal with the potatoes. Carefully add the potatoes to the skillet. Cover and cook for 15 minutes, turning often and scraping the bottom of the pan.

Uncover and continue to cook and turn for 10 minutes more or until browned to your liking. Serves 4.

Calories—176; Saturated fat—0 g.; Total fat—3 g.; Carbohydrates—34 g.; Cholesterol—0 mg.; Sodium—452 mg.

YAM CRISPIES

PAREVE

What a source of Vitamin A for the kids!

Cooking spray   **3 medium yams, thinly sliced**

Preheat the oven to 400 degrees.

Coat a nonstick baking sheet with the cooking spray. Arrange the yam slices on the baking sheet and coat them with the cooking spray.

Bake in the oven for 10-15 minutes, turning once as they brown.

Variation: Try slicing beets or carrots. Serves 6.

Calories—21; Saturated fat—0 g.; Total fat—2 g.; Carbohydrates—0 g.; Cholesterol—0 mg.; Sodium—0 mg.;

OVEN FRIES

PAREVE

Olive oil cooking spray
4 medium potatoes, cut into 1-
   inch wedges
1½ tsp. paprika

1 tsp. onion powder
½ tsp. garlic powder
¼ tsp. salt (optional)

Preheat the oven to 400 degrees.

Lightly coat a nonstick baking sheet with the cooking spray. Arrange the potato wedges on a baking sheet in a single layer. Lightly coat the tops of the potato wedges with the cooking spray.

Mix the seasonings and sprinkle the desired amount over the wedges. Bake for 40 minutes or until lightly browned and crispy. Serve with Low Sodium Catsup if desired. Serves 4-5.

Calories—174; Saturated fat—0 g.; Total fat—0 g.; Carbohydrates—39 g.; Cholesterol—0 mg.; Sodium—55 mg.

LOW-SODIUM CATSUP

PAREVE

If you need to watch your salt intake, this is quick and easy to make.

½ cup low-sodium tomato puree
2 tbsp. apple juice concentrate

1 tbsp. apple cider vinegar
⅛ tsp. ground cloves

Combine all of the ingredients and chill. Makes ½ cup.

Per 1 tbsp. serving: Calories—8; Saturated fat—0 g.; Total fat—0 g.; Carbohydrates—2 g.; Cholesterol—0 mg.; Sodium—4 mg.

Kugels and Tzimmes

POTATO KUGEL

PAREVE

5 heaping cups well-scrubbed
   potatoes, finely grated
2 large onions, grated
3 egg whites
3 tbsp. matzah meal

1/4 tsp. salt
1/2 tsp. black pepper
1 tbsp. oil
Cooking spray

Preheat the oven to 375 degrees. Heat the baking dish while preparing the kugel.

In a bowl, mix together the potatoes, onions, egg whites, matzah meal, salt, and pepper.

Add the oil to the baking dish and heat through for 1-2 minutes more. Spoon the potato mixture into the dish. It will sizzle. Lightly coat the top of the potato mixture with the cooking spray. Bake for 1 hour or until golden brown. Serves 6.

Calories—219; Saturated fat—0 g.; Total fat—3 g.; Carbohydrates—42 mg.; Cholesterol—0 mg.; Sodium—136 mg.

SWEET DAIRY PASSOVER NOODLE KUGEL

DAIRY

When looking for a noodle kugel to adapt, I came across this traditionally flavored kugel from my husband's grandmother, the late Helen Lettas.

1 12-oz. pkg. egg yolk-free,
   kosher-for-Passover noodles
Cooking spray
1 cup Passover egg substitute
12 oz. lowfat cottage cheese
1 apple, peeled and grated

1 cup crushed pineapple, drained
3 tbsp. sugar or 3 tbsp. apple
   juice concentrate
1/3 cup raisins or 1/4 cup Apricot-
   Pineapple Jam
Cinnamon

Preheat the oven to 375 degrees.

Cook the noodles according to package directions. Drain in a colander and rinse with cold water.

Coat a baking dish with the cooking spray.

In a bowl, mix together the noodles, egg substitute, cottage cheese, apple, pineapple, sugar, and raisins. Turn into the baking dish. Sprinkle the cinnamon over the top. Bake in the preheated oven for 375 degrees for 40 minutes or until the top is golden brown. Serves 6-8.

Calories—243; Saturated fat—0 g.; Total fat—1 g.; Carbohydrates—56 g.; Cholesterol—2 mg.; Sodium—227 mg.

MIXED VEGETABLE KUGEL

PAREVE

1 cup carrots, grated
1 large onion, grated
1 lb. asparagus, tough ends
   removed
2 lb. spinach, cleaned and
   steamed, or 2 10-oz. pkgs.
   frozen spinach

3 egg whites
2 tbsp. matzah meal (optional)
1/4 tsp. salt
1/4 tsp. black pepper
1/8 tsp. dry dillweed
Cooking spray

Preheat the oven to 350 degrees.

Combine the carrots and onion in a large bowl.

In a large skillet, steam the asparagus and spinach until asparagus is tender-crisp and the spinach is wilted. Drain the spinach and finely chop in a food processor. Remove, then chop the asparagus and mix both into the carrots and onion. Blend in the egg whites, matzah meal, salt, pepper, and dillweed.

Coat a 9-by-9-inch casserole dish with the cooking spray. Spoon the kugel mixture in evenly and bake for 1 hour or until the top is golden and kugel is set. Serves 6.

Calories—104; Saturated fat—0 g.; Total fat—1 g.; Carbohydrates—15 g.; Cholesterol—0 mg.; Sodium—259 mg.

APPLE MATZAH KUGEL

PAREVE

5 apples, peeled, grated
⅓ cup matzah meal
¼ cup Passover egg substitute
½ cup sugar
¼ cup apple juice

3 tbsp. lemon juice
1½ tsp. cinnamon
5 egg whites
Cooking spray
Cinnamon for topping

Preheat the oven to 350 degrees.

In a bowl, combine the first 7 ingredients.

In a separate bowl, beat the egg whites until stiff and fold into the apple mixture.

Coat a baking dish with the cooking spray. Turn the mixture in. Sprinkle some cinnamon over the top and bake for 45 minutes until the top is lightly brown. Serves 6.

Calories—222; Saturated fat—0 g.; Total fat—1 g.; Carbohydrates—49 g.; Cholesterol—0 mg.; Sodium—62 mg.

QUICK ITALIAN-FLAVORED TOMATO KUGEL

DAIRY

4 matzahs, broken up
3½ cups canned whole tomatoes, undrained
1 cup mushrooms, sliced
1 small onion, chopped
2 tsp. basil

2 tsp. oregano
Dash cayenne pepper, or to taste
2 egg whites
Cooking spray
4 oz. of any kind of lowfat white or yellow cheese, shredded

Preheat the oven to 375 degrees.

In a bowl, combine the matzah with the canned tomatoes and juice. Break up the tomatoes. Add the mushrooms, onion, basil, oregano, and cayenne pepper.

Beat the egg whites until stiff peaks form and fold into the matzah mixture. Coat a baking dish with the cooking spray and spoon in the mixture. Bake for 35 minutes. Spread the cheese over the top and bake for 10 minutes more or until the cheese melts. Serves 6.

Calories—177; Saturated fat—2 g.; Total fat—4 g.; Carbohydrates—27 g.; Cholesterol—11 mg.; Sodium—127 mg.

CARROT KUGEL

The traditional flavor of this kugel is not lost
with the lack of egg yolks and oil.

2 cups carrots, thinly sliced
1 cup chicken broth
1 tsp. oil
¼ cup matzah meal
1 cup onion, minced

1 tbsp. parsley, finely chopped
1 tsp. salt
⅛ tsp. black pepper
2 egg whites
Cooking spray

Preheat the oven to 350 degrees.

Cook the carrots until tender. Mash them and add the broth, oil, matzah meal, onion, parsley, salt, and pepper.

In another bowl, beat the egg whites until stiff but not dry. Fold into the carrot mixture.

Spray a baking dish with the cooking spray. Turn the mixture into the dish. Bake in the preheated oven for 50-60 minutes. Serves 6.

Calories—85; Saturated fat—0 g.; Total fat—2 g.; Carbohydrates—14 g.; Cholesterol—0 mg.; Sodium—142 mg.

PINEAPPLE KUGEL

PAREVE

4 matzahs
2 cups orange juice
½ cup dried apricots, snipped in half
1 20-oz. can unsweetened crushed pineapple, drained

(reserve juice)
¼ cup sugar (optional)
1 tsp. cinnamon
4 egg whites
Cooking spray

Preheat the oven to 350 degrees.

In a large bowl, break up the matzahs, pour the orange juice over them, and let stand for about 10 minutes.

In a small saucepan, cover the snipped apricots with the reserved pineapple juice and cook over low heat for about 10 minutes to plump up. Drain the orange juice from the matzahs and squeeze dry. Drain the pineapple juice from the apricots and combine the apricots with the matzahs. Stir in the crushed pineapple, sugar, and ¾ teaspoon of the cinnamon and mix well.

In a bowl, beat the egg whites until stiff peaks form but not dry. Fold in the beaten egg whites. Coat an 11-by-9-inch baking dish with the cooking spray and spoon the mixture into it. Sprinkle the top with the remaining ¼ teaspoon of cinnamon and bake in the preheated oven for 50 minutes. Serves 6.

Calories—142; Saturated fat—0 g.; Total fat—0 g.; Carbohydrates—31 g.; Cholesterol—0 mg.; Sodium—40 mg.

ZUCCHINI SQUASH KUGEL

PAREVE

3 cups grated zucchini squash
1 small onion, grated
1 cup grated carrot
2 egg whites

⅓ cup matzah meal
1 tbsp. white horseradish
⅛ tsp. black pepper
Cooking spray

Preheat the oven to 350 degrees.

In a bowl, mix all of the ingredients (except the cooking spray) well.

Coat a 9-by-9-inch baking pan with the cooking spray and spoon in the mixture. Bake in the preheated oven for about 50 minutes. Serves 6-8.

Calories—51; Saturated fat—0 g.; Total fat—0 g.; Carbohydrates—9 g.; Cholesterol—0 mg.; Sodium—91 mg.

CAULIFLOWER KUGEL

DAIRY

1 head cauliflower, cut into
   florets
Cooking spray
1 large onion, chopped
1 large stalk celery

¼ cup Parmesan cheese
¼ tsp. dried dill
⅛ tsp. black pepper
1½ tbsp. cake meal
3 egg whites

Preheat the oven to 350 degrees.

Steam the cauliflower until tender.

Meanwhile, coat a saute pan with the cooking spray and over medium-high heat, saute the onion until lightly browned.

Mash the cauliflower and mix in the remaining ingredients.

Spray a 9-by-9-inch baking pan with the cooking spray. Transfer the kugel into the baking pan. Bake in the preheated oven for 50 minutes until a lightly golden brown. Serves 6.

Calories—48; Saturated fat—1 g.; Total fat—1 g.; Carbohydrates—6 g.; Cholesterol—2 mg.; Sodium—90 mg.

TZIMMES TZOUFFLE

I created this dish years ago in my early days of being health conscious. There's never been a need to update this recipe.

1½ lb. sweet potatoes
¼ cup water
3 carrots, sliced
2 apples, sliced
1½ tsp. lemon peel, grated

¼ cup apple, orange, or pineapple juice concentrate, thawed
2 egg whites, beaten into soft peaks
Cooking spray

Preheat the oven to the 350 degrees.

Bake the sweet potatoes. Cool. Peel and mash. Set aside.

In a saucepan, combine the water, carrots, and apples. Cover and cook over medium heat until tender. Drain and mash.

Combine the carrot mixture with the potatoes. Mix in the juice concentrate and lemon peel.

Beat the egg whites until soft peaks form. Fold into the tzimmes. Coat an 8-by-8-inch casserole dish with the cooking spray and turn the mixture evenly into it and bake in the preheated oven for 30-35 minutes. Serves 4.

Calories—280; Saturated fat—0 g.; Total fat—1 g.; Carbohydrates—62 g.; Cholesterol—0 mg.; Sodium—69 mg.

CANDIED SWEET POTATO TZIMMES

PAREVE

4 medium sweet potatoes
4 canned peach halves, drained
   and sliced
¼ cup maple syrup
¾ cup orange juice
¼ tsp. cinnamon

¼ tsp. ginger
1 tsp. orange peel, finely grated
1 tsp. potato starch
1 tbsp. pecans, finely chopped
   (optional)

Preheat the oven to 375 degrees.

Slice the sweet potatoes into ½-inch slices and steam until tender. In a casserole dish, layer the sweet potatoes with the peaches.

In a small bowl, combine the maple syrup, orange juice, cinnamon, ginger, orange peel, and potato starch. Pour over the sweet potatoes and peaches. Sprinkle the pecans over the mixture. Bake uncovered for about 20 minutes or until the sauce is bubbly. Serves 4-6.

Calories—155; Saturated fat—0 g.; Total fat—0 g.; Carbohydrates—36 g.; Cholesterol—0 mg.; Sodium—12 mg.

Fruit

FRESH FRUIT SALAD

PAREVE

2 small green apples, cubed
1 cup pineapple chunks
2 kiwis, peeled and cubed
1 papaya, peeled and cut into chunks
2 medium bananas, peeled and sliced

3 cups strawberries, cleaned and cut into bite-sized pieces
¼ cup pineapple juice
Juice of ½ lime
⅛ tsp. powdered ginger

In a bowl, combine the fruits. Mix the pineapple juice, lime juice, and ginger together and pour over the fruit. Chill. Serves 6-8.

Calories—128; Saturated fat—0 g.; Total fat—1 g.; Carbohydrates—29 g.; Cholesterol—0 mg.; Sodium—4 mg.

PRUNE COMPOTE WITH ORANGE

PAREVE

1 12-oz. pkg. pitted prunes
3 cups apple juice
1 3-inch cinnamon stick

Peel of 1 orange
2 oranges, peeled and sectioned
1 banana, sliced

In a saucepan, add the prunes, apple juice, cinnamon stick, and orange peel. Bring to a boil, reduce heat to low, cover, and simmer for 15 minutes.

Remove from heat. Cool. Slice the orange sections in half if they are large and add to prunes. Add the bananas when it's ready to serve so they keep their freshness. Serves 6.

Calories—195; Saturated fat—0 g.; Total fat—1 g.; Carbohydrates—45 g.; Cholesterol—0 mg.; Sodium—11 mg.

SPICED POACHED APPLES

4 apples or pears, peeled and
  halved
1 orange, sliced, then sliced
  again in half-moons
1½ cups apple juice

½ cup red sweet wine
½ tsp. cinnamon
3 whole cloves
¼ tsp. fresh ginger, grated
2 cups raspberries

Place the apples or pears in a skillet and alternate with the orange slices.

Combine the remaining ingredients except for the raspberries and pour over the apples. Bring to a boil, reduce heat, cover pan, and simmer for 20 minutes or until fruit is tender.

Serve warm or chilled apple halves with a spoonful of the raspberries and the juice. Discard the oranges if desired. Serves 8.

Calories—166; Saturated fat—0 g.; Total fat—0 g.; Carbohydrates—36 g.; Cholesterol—0 mg.; Sodium—4 mg.

PEAR BLUEBERRY CRISP

5 pears, unpeeled and sliced
1½ cups blueberries
1 tsp. cinnamon

¼ tsp. nutmeg
¼ tsp. powdered ginger
½ cup apple juice

Preheat the oven to 350 degrees.

In a mixing bowl, toss the pears and blueberries with the spices and arrange in a baking dish. Drizzle the apple juice all around the fruit. Sprinkle Crumb Topping (recipe follows) over the fruit. Bake in the preheated oven for 30 minutes or until the topping lightly browns. It is best served warm. Try serving with Creamy Whipped Topping.

CRUMB TOPPING

½ cup matzah meal
2 tbsp. potato starch
½ tsp. cinnamon

3 tbsp. sugar
1 tbsp. apple juice concentrate
1 tbsp. oil

In a bowl, combine all of the ingredients and mix well. Serves 6-8.

Variation: Substitute apples or peaches for pears.

Calories—87; Saturated fat—0 g.; Total fat—1 g.; Carbohydrates—20 g.; Cholesterol—0 mg.; Sodium—3 mg.

PINEAPPLE STREUSEL BAKED APPLES

PAREVE

¼ cup matzah meal
⅓ cup canned crushed pineapple,
   undrained
½ tsp. cinnamon
¼ tsp. nutmeg

4 baking apples
2 dates sliced in half
4 3-inch cinnamon sticks
1 cup pineapple juice

Preheat the oven to 350 degrees.

In a small bowl, mix the matzah meal, crushed pineapple, cinnamon, and nutmeg. Set aside.

Core the apples and peel the skin around the top of each apple. Fill each apple cavity with the matzah meal mixture. Push each date halfway into the center of the filling. Push each cinnamon stick into the side of each filled core.

Place in a baking dish. Pour the pineapple juice over the apples. Bake in the preheated oven for about 50 minutes, basting occasionally until the apples are soft and the juice thickens. Serves 4.

Calories—214; Saturated fat—0 g.; Total fat—1 g.; Carbohydrates—50 g.; Cholesterol—0 mg.; Sodium—1 mg.

BLUEBERRY BANANA SLUSH

PAREVE

½ **cup blueberries, frozen**
½ **cup orange juice**
½ **banana**

½ **cup ice cubes**
½ **tsp. vanilla**

Puree the blueberries and orange juice. Add the remaining ingredients and process until slushy. Serves 1-2.

Calories—123; Saturated fat—0 g.; Total fat—0 g.; Carbohydrates—28 g.; Cholesterol—0 mg.; Sodium—2 mg.

PINEAPPLE SLUSH

PAREVE

*My daughter Jennifer asks for this treat often. It is so easy to make.
It's a fast throw-together for an afternoon or evening snack.
You'll want to eat it with a spoon.*

⅓ **cup crushed pineapple, undrained**
2 **tbsp. orange juice concentrate**

About 1 cup ice
2 fresh mint leaves

Puree all of the ingredients in a blender. Don't over-blend! Makes 1 delicious healthy serving.

Variation: Substitute the fruit of your choice for the pineapple.

Calories—121; Saturated fat—0 g.; Total fat—0 g.; Carbohydrates—30 g.; Cholesterol—0 mg.; Sodium—8 mg.

STRAWBERRY-APPLE SAUCE

PAREVE

So naturally sweet you can serve it for dessert.

2 cups apples, cored and sliced   **2 cups frozen strawberries**

In a soup pot, combine the ingredients and simmer for about 20 minutes or until the apples are soft. Puree the mixture to a consistency of your liking.

You may also combine blueberries, peaches, or raspberries with the apples. Makes 2 cups.

Calories—65; Saturated fat—0 g.; Total fat—0 g.; Carbohydrates—15 g.; Cholesterol—0 mg.; Sodium—1 mg.

Note: To serve as a dessert, add a dollop of yogurt.

CANDIED FRUIT BALLS

PAREVE

A delicious high-fiber candy.

CANDY

1 cup dry apricots	2½ tbsp. cocoa
1 cup pitted dates	⅓ cup chopped pecans
1 cup raisins	2 tbsp. any Passover liqueur,
1 recipe Orange-Flavored Matzah	Slivovitz, or sweet red wine

In a food processor or grinder, process the candy ingredients until well blended and smooth. Roll into 1-inch balls.

COATING

2 tbsp. sugar   **½ tsp. potato starch**

On a plate, mix the sugar and potato starch. Roll the balls into the mixture. Store in a container and chill. Makes 2 dozen.

Per ball: Calories—81; Saturated fat—0 g.; Total fat—1 g.; Carbohydrates—15 g.; Cholesterol—0 mg.; Sodium—5 mg.

ORANGE-FLAVORED MATZAH

PAREVE

2½ matzahs, crumbled
2½ tbsp. orange juice concentrate

1½ tsp. cinnamon
Cooking spray

In a bowl, mix matzah, orange juice concentrate and cinnamon until matzah is coated. Coat a nonstick skillet with cooking spray. Over medium heat, stir mixture continuously 3 minutes or until matzah pieces are lightly toasted. Makes 8 2-tablespoon servings.

Serving suggestion: Sprinkle over yogurt, Prune Compote with Orange, or a fruit cup of your choice.

Calories—38; Saturated fat—0 g.; Total fat—0 g.; Carbohydrates—8 g.; Cholesterol—0 mg.; Sodium—0 mg.

Desserts

PINEAPPLE LIME SORBET

PAREVE

A deliteful, refreshing way to end a meal.

2 cups fresh pineapple, peeled and cut into chunks

1 cup honeydew melon, peeled and cut into chunks

3 tbsp. lime juice (juice of 1 lime)

¼ cup pineapple juice concentrate

¼ cup sugar

4 sprigs mint leaves for garnish

In a food processor or blender puree all of the ingredients.

Pour into a metal bowl, cover, and freeze until the sorbet has solidified. Twenty minutes or so before serving, break the sorbet into chunks and place them in a food processor. Process the chunks until just smooth and serve. If the sorbet is over-processed, return to the chilled bowl and freeze for about 15 minutes.

Serving suggestion: Serve this with Fresh Fruit Salad topped with Pineapple Sauce. Garnish with a mint leaf. It's a real treat. Makes approximately 1 pint.

Per ½-cup serving: Calories—118; Saturated fat—0 g.; Total fat—0 g.; Carbohydrates—27 g.; Cholesterol—0 mg.; Sodium—19 mg.

CINNAMON CHOCOLATE CAKE ROLL

DAIRY

This is an elegant-looking dessert. It is just right for that light but sweet taste people want after a big meal. I recommend it as dessert with a vegetarian seder. Even my kids say this doesn't taste Pesadige. It's everyone's favorite!

MOCHA CREAM FILLING

¾ cup nonfat dry milk
¼ cup ice water
¾ tsp. instant decaffeinated
   coffee crystals
1 tsp. vanilla extract

Dash cinnamon
2 tbsp. sugar
3 tbsp. water
½ tbsp. unflavored kosher
   gelatin

Chill a medium glass bowl and beaters.

In the chilled bowl, combine ½ cup of the dry milk, the ice water, instant coffee, vanilla extract, and cinnamon. Beat at high speed for 3 minutes. Add the remaining dry milk and the sugar and continue beating 2 minutes more. The mixture will double in volume.

In a small microwave-safe bowl, heat the water to just boiling. Blend in the gelatin and mix quickly to smooth out lumps. Add the gelatin mixture to the cream filling and beat 3 minutes more. The mixture will be slightly glossy. Chill 30 minutes before using. Makes 1½ cups.

CAKE ROLL

¼ cup cake meal
¼ cup cocoa
½ tsp. cinnamon
5 egg whites
⅔ cups sugar

2 tbsp. water
1 tsp. vanilla
2-3 tbsp. sugar
3 strawberries, sliced, for garnish

Preheat the oven to 375 degrees.

Grease a foil-lined 10-by-15-inch baking sheet.

In a bowl, stir the cake meal, cocoa, and cinnamon together.

In a medium bowl, beat the egg whites until soft peaks form. Gradually add the sugar, water, and vanilla. Fold in the cake meal mixture a third at a time until well blended.

Spread the batter evenly to edges of the baking pan. Bake for 10-12 minutes or until the roll springs back to the touch.

Invert onto a dish towel sprinkled lightly with sugar. Using a sharp knife, carefully loosen all around the sides first. Then, going in one direction, keep separating the cake roll from the foil with the knife. Immediately roll the cake and towel into a cylindrical shape, starting with the long edge. Cool on a rack.

Unroll the cake roll. Stir the Mocha Cream Filling and spread evenly over the cake. Reroll, wrap in plastic wrap, and refrigerate for minimum of 4 hours. To serve, trim the uneven edges and slice into 1-inch portions. Garnish with the strawberry slices. Serves 6-8.

Calories—64; Saturated fat—0 g.; Total fat—0 g.; Carbohydrates—9 g.; Cholesterol—1 mg.; Sodium—95 mg.

CHOCOLATE RASPBERRY PUDDING

DAIRY

A quick haimeshe *dessert.*

1 pkg. Passover instant chocolate pudding mix (use sugar-free if available)
1½ cups cold skim milk

1½ tbsp. raspberry preserves (use sugar-free if available)
1 cup plain nonfat yogurt

In a medium bowl, sprinkle the pudding mix over the milk. On your mixer's lowest speed, beat for 30 seconds. Combine the raspberry preserves and yogurt and add to the pudding mixture. Beat for 30 seconds more or until thickened. Pour into dessert dishes and chill before serving.

Variation: For Chocolate Mocha Pudding, omit the raspberry preserves and mix 1½ teaspoons of instant decaffeinated coffee granules into the yogurt. Then continue with the above instructions. Serves 4.

Calories—176; Saturated fat—0 g.; Total fat—1 g.; Carbohydrates—35 g.; Cholesterol—3 mg.; Sodium—187 mg.

BERRY FROZEN YOGURT

¼ cup apple juice concentrate,
warmed
2 tsp. kosher gelatin
3 cups strawberries
1 cup blueberries

1 cup raspberries
½ cup sugar
2½ cups nonfat plain yogurt
2-3 tbsp. liqueur or sweet wine

In a small bowl, combine the apple juice concentrate and gelatin. Stir to dissolve. Set aside.

In a food processor, puree the remaining ingredients. Blend in the gelatin mixture and freeze.

To serve frozen yogurt later or next day, break into chunks and process until smooth. Serves 8.

Calories—167; Saturated fat—0 g.; Total fat—0 g.; Carbohydrates—34 g.; Cholesterol—1 mg.; Sodium—58 mg.

INSTANT RASPBERRY SORBET

This is a quick-fix dessert and is best served right away.

2 cups frozen raspberries

½ cup apple juice concentrate

Place the raspberries in a blender running at high speed. Add the apple juice concentrate for desired consistency of sorbet. Serve immediately or store in the freezer several hours before serving.

Note: If the sorbet is frozen solid, let it sit out for a while or soften it for a few seconds in the microwave. Then process again before serving. Serves 3-4.

Calories—137; Saturated fat—0 g.; Total fat—0 g.; Carbohydrates—33 g.; Cholesterol—0 mg.; Sodium—4 mg.

NO-CHOLESTEROL CHOCOLATE CHIFFON CAKE

PAREVE

Enjoy the convenience of a cake mix without the high fat and cholesterol!

1 Passover Chocolate Chiffon Cake mix
1½ tbsp. instant decaffeinated coffee granules

⅓ cup water
½ cup mashed banana
6 egg whites

Preheat the oven to 350 degrees.

In a large bowl, empty the cake mix and make a well in the center. Add the coffee granules, water, and mashed banana. Beat at medium speed with an electric mixer for 2 minutes.

In a separate bowl, beat the egg whites until stiff peaks form. Carefully fold the egg whites into the chocolate-banana mixture. Pour into a greased 9-inch Bundt pan or springform pan.

Bake in the preheated oven for 50-60 minutes or until the cake springs back to the touch. Remove from oven and invert the pan onto the cooling rack. Cool.

Serving suggestion: Serve with Creamy Whipped Topping with a diced banana in it. Serves 8.

Calories—148; Saturated fat—0 g.; Total fat—3 g.; Carbohydrates—27 g.; Cholesterol—0 mg.; Sodium—167 mg.

COCOA MERINGUES

I make some version of these cookies every year at my seder.
This is only my latest version. It's just the sweetness everyone needs
without being a filling dessert.
Of course, they're just as good without the cereal.

½ cup Manischewitz Crispy Os
   cereal (cocoa-flavored) or
   Fruities cereal
1½ tbsp. unsweetened cocoa
⅓ cup sugar

¼ tsp. cinnamon, optional
3 egg whites
3 oz. semisweet chocolate,
   coarsely grated

Preheat the oven to 300 degrees.

In a plastic bag, crush the chocolate cereal coarsely between two sheets of waxed paper with a glass or a rolling pin.

In a small bowl, combine the cocoa, sugar, and cinnamon. Set aside.

In a glass or metal bowl, beat the egg whites until soft peaks form. Gradually add the cocoa mixture until well blended. Fold in the cereal and grated chocolate and drop by heaping teaspoonfuls on a nonstick cookie sheet. Bake in the preheated oven for 20 minutes. Turn off the oven and leave the cookies in for 1 hour. Remove from the oven and cool. Makes approximately 3½ dozen delicious, bite-sized cookies.

Per cookie: Calories—14; Saturated fat—0 g.; Total fat—0 g.; Carbohydrates—2 g.; Cholesterol—0 mg.; Sodium—7 mg.

GOLDEN MACAROONS

*Macaroons are traditional during Pesach.
This is a healthier twist on tradition. The carrots substitute
for the texture of the high-fat shredded coconut.*

**½ cup almonds, ground in a food
processor**
1 cup carrots, finely shredded
½ cup cake meal

½ cup sugar
1 tsp. almond extract
3 egg whites
Cooking spray

Preheat the oven to 350 degrees.

In a bowl combine all of the ingredients. Spoon by heaping teaspoonfuls onto a nonstick cookie sheet that has been coated with the cooking spray. Bake for 20 minutes or until the cookies are a light golden brown. Makes approximately 1½ dozen.

Per cookie: Calories—53; Saturated fat—0 g.; Total fat—2 g.; Carbohydrates—7 g.; Cholesterol—0 mg.; Sodium—12 mg.

CHEESECAKE

Light in texture, rich in taste.

CRUST

⅓ cup matzah meal   1½ tbsp. oil
1½ tbsp. sugar

Preheat the oven to 350 degrees.
Combine all of the ingredients and lightly press into a 9-inch springform pan.

FILLING

16 oz. lowfat cottage cheese   1½ tsp. lemon, vanilla, or
1 cup nonfat plain yogurt   almond extract
3 tbsp. potato starch   4 egg whites
½ cup maple syrup

Blend all of the ingredients except the egg whites for 2 minutes or until smooth.
Beat the egg whites until stiff peaks form but not dry. Fold into the cheesecake filling mixture and turn into the springform pan. Bake in the preheated oven for 1 hour.
Reduce the heat to 300 degrees and bake for 15 minutes longer. Cool completely and refrigerate for about 4 hours or overnight.
Garnish with fresh fruit such as strawberries or kiwifruit and top with the Fruit Glaze. Serves 8.

FRUIT GLAZE

½ tsp. unflavored kosher gelatin   ½ cup pureed fruit: peaches,
2 tbsp. frozen pineapple juice   strawberries, or blueberries
   concentrate, thawed

In a small saucepan, sprinkle the gelatin over the pineapple juice concentrate and let it stand for 1 minute to soften. Then stir over low heat to completely dissolve. Mix in the pureed fruit and pour over cooled cheesecake. Chill until the glaze is set.

Calories—215; Saturated fat—1 g.; Total fat—3 g.; Carbohydrates—36 g.; Cholesterol—3 mg.; Sodium—275 mg.

STRAWBERRY ANGEL FOOD CAKE

PAREVE

½ cup cake meal
½ cup potato starch
1 cup sugar
11 egg whites, room temperature

2 tsp. almond or vanilla extract
1½ cups strawberries, stems
  removed
1 pint strawberries for garnish

Preheat the oven to 325 degrees.

In a bowl, combine the cake meal, potato starch, and ½ of the sugar. Have a flour sifter ready.

In a bowl, beat the egg whites until foamy, add the almond extract and continue to beat until stiff peaks form. Slowly add the remaining sugar until peaks turn glossy. Crush or puree ½ cup of the strawberries and fold into the whites. Sift and fold the cake meal mixture into the whites. Dice the remaining strawberries and fold into batter.

Spoon the mixture into an ungreased 10-inch tube pan. Bake for 1 hour or until the cake springs back when touched. Remove cake from oven and invert onto a cooling rack or a wine bottle, permitting air to circulate while cooling thoroughly (2-3 hours).

Loosen sides and center of the tube with a knife. Invert onto a cake platter. To garnish, slice enough strawberries to fan out around cake. Place whole strawberries into center of cake. Serves 8.

Serving suggestion: Serve with Strawberry Sauce or Creamy Whipped Topping for a dairy dessert.

Variation: Add 2 teaspoons of Passover sugar-free strawberry-flavored kosher gelatin to the potato starch and cake meal mixture. This gives the cake a richer pink color.

Cake without sauce: Calories—172; Saturated fat—0 g.; Total fat—0 g.; Carbohydrates—37 g.; Cholesterol—0 mg.; Sodium—80 mg.

PINEAPPLE SAUCE

2 cups pineapple juice
¼ cup orange juice
1 tbsp. potato starch

2 tbsp. Pina Coconetta or other
   sweet Passover wine (optional)

In a saucepan over medium heat, combine all of the ingredients, and stir until the mixture slightly thickens. Makes 2 cups.

Per ¼-cup serving: Calories—50; Saturated fat—0 g.; Total fat—0 g.; Carbohydrates—11 g.; Cholesterol—0 mg.; Sodium—2 mg.

STRAWBERRY SAUCE

2 pints strawberries, hulled
3 tbsp. fruit juice concentrate
   (apple, orange, or pineapple)

1-2 tbsp. Manischewitz Pina
   Coconetta or sweet red
   Passover wine, or to taste

Puree the strawberries; add the fruit juice concentrate and Pina Coconetta to sweeten. Chill before serving. Makes 2 cups.

Per ¼-cup serving: Calories—26; Saturated fat—0 g.; Total fat—0 g.; Carbohydrates—5 g.; Cholesterol—0 mg.; Sodium—1 mg.

PINEAPPLE ORANGE CAKE

PAREVE

¼ cup pineapple juice concentrate, thawed
¼ cup orange juice concentrate, thawed
1 cup potato starch

1 cup pineapple, crushed
11 egg whites
¾ cup sugar
Peel of 1 orange, grated (approx. 2 tbsp.)

Preheat the oven to 325 degrees.

In a small bowl, combine the juice concentrates. Set aside. In a second small bowl, have the measured-out potato starch. In a third small bowl, the crushed pineapple.

In a large bowl, beat the egg whites until foamy. Gradually add the sugar while beating the egg whites until glossy soft peaks form. With a mixer set on low, blend in the potato starch.

With a spoon, blend in the juice concentrates, crushed pineapple, and grated orange peel.

Spoon the batter evenly into an ungreased 10-inch tube pan. Bake for 50 minutes or until the cake springs back when touched and is lightly golden brown. Remove the cake from the oven and invert onto a cooling rack or wine bottle, which will permit the air to circulate while cooling thoroughly. Loosen the sides and center of the pan with a knife and unmold onto a cake platter. Serves 8.

Serving suggestion: Serve with the Pineapple Sauce.

Calories—193; Saturated fat—0 g.; Total fat—0 g.; Carbohydrates—41 g.; Cholesterol—0 mg.; Sodium—38 mg.

BANANA CARROT CAKE

PAREVE/DAIRY

½ cup bananas, mashed
1½ cups carrots, very finely
  grated
¼ cup ground almonds

1½ tsp. vanilla extract
½ cup sugar
¾ cup cake meal
6 egg whites

Preheat the oven 350 degrees.

In a bowl mix the bananas, carrots, almonds, vanilla, and sugar. Blend in the cake meal.

In a separate bowl, beat the egg whites until stiff (but not dry) peaks form. Carefully fold into the carrot mixture a little at a time until well blended. Turn into an 8-by-8½-inch springform pan.

Bake in the preheated oven for 40 minutes or until the knife comes out clean from the center. Serves 6.

Serving suggestion: Serve with Pineapple Sauce, or heat a little Pineapple-Apricot Jam and spread it over the cooled cake. If you are serving a dairy meal, blend ½ cup dry cottage cheese, ½ cup lowfat cottage cheese, 1 tsp. vanilla, and spread over the jam as a cream-cheese frosting. Serves 6.

Calories—213; Saturated fat—1 g.; Total fat—9 g.; Carbohydrates—26 g.; Cholesterol—0 mg.; Sodium—66 mg.

WINE CAKE

¾ **cup cake meal**
2 **tsp. cinnamon**
1 **tsp. Paskesz Passover baking**
  powder (optional)
10 **egg whites**

¾ **cup sugar**
½ **cup sweet red wine**
¼ **cup chopped nuts**
Cooking oil

Preheat the oven to 350 degrees.

In a bowl, combine the cake meal, cinnamon, and baking powder.

Beat the egg whites until frothy. Gradually add the sugar while beating until peaks form. Alternately fold in the cake meal mixture and wine until well blended. Fold in the nuts.

Wipe a bundt pan with the cooking oil. Spoon the cake mixture in smoothly. Bake in the preheated oven for 30-40 minutes or until the cake is lightly browned. Loosen the sides with a knife. Cool. Invert onto cake platter. Serves 8-10.

Serving suggestion: Serve with Wine Sauce.

Calories—58; Saturated fat—0 g.; Total fat—2 g.; Carbohydrates—3 mg.; Cholesterol—0 mg.; Sodium—91 mg.

WINE SAUCE

PAREVE

1 cup sweet red wine
¼ cup sugar
¼ cup orange juice or lemon juice

1 tbsp. lemon juice
1 tbsp. potato starch

In a saucepan over medium heat, combine the wine and sugar. Blend in the orange juice, lemon juice, and potato starch and add to the saucepan. Stir until the mixture thickens slightly. Serves 8-10.

Serving suggestions: Serve warm or chilled on Wine Cake. Try Fresh Fruit Salad spooned over Wine Cake or Pineapple Orange Cake and top it with Wine Sauce.

Calories—64; Saturated fat—0 g.; Total fat—0 g.; Carbohydrates—9 g.; Cholesterol—0 mg.; Sodium—3 mg.

SUNSHINE MOUSSE

PAREVE

2 oranges, peeled and sectioned
2 tbsp. lemon juice
¼ cup orange juice concentrate
¼ cup sugar

1 tbsp. unflavored kosher gelatin
¼ cup water
2 egg whites
2 tbsp. sugar

In a food processor puree the oranges, lemon juice, and orange juice concentrate. Remove ½ cup of the puree.

In a saucepan, over medium heat, stir together the sugar, gelatin, and water with the ½ cup of puree. Stir until the gelatin is dissolved. Remove from heat and stir in the remaining puree. Chill thoroughly for about 2 hours.

In a medium bowl, beat the egg whites while gradually adding the sugar until soft peaks form. Gently fold the fruit mixture into the egg whites. Spoon into five dessert cups. Chill again before serving. Serves 5.

Calories—127; Saturated fat—0 g.; Total fat—0 g.; Carbohydrates—27 g.; Cholesterol—0 mg.; Sodium—25 mg.

CREAMY WHIPPED TOPPING

Adding the gelatin makes the cream more substantial and longer lasting.

1 tsp. unflavored kosher gelatin
3 tbsp. hot water
1 cup nonfat dry milk
½ cup ice water or ice-cold apple
   juice

2 tsp. vanilla
1 tsp. lemon juice
2 tbsp. sugar (or sugar substitute)

Chill a medium glass bowl and beaters.

In a small bowl stir together the kosher gelatine and the hot water until the kosher gelatine is dissolved. Set aside.

In the chilled bowl, combine the dry milk, ice water, vanilla, and lemon juice. Beat at high speed for 5 minutes while gradually beating in the sugar. Mixture will thicken and double in volume.

Add the kosher gel mix in a slow steady stream to the whipped mixture, while beating for 3 minutes longer. The cream will thicken more and stiffen slightly. Chill for 30 minutes before serving. Makes 2⅓ cups.

Per 2-tbsp. serving: Calories—28; Saturated fat—0 g.; Total fat—0 g.; Carbohydrates—6 g.; Cholesterol—1 mg.; Sodium—33 mg.

INDEX